Money Skills for Teens
The Ultimate Teen Guide to Personal Finance and Making Cents of Your Dollars

Jessica Blakely

ISBN: 978-0-473-70277-9 (Kindle)

ISBN: 978-0-473-70275-5 (Paperback)

ISBN: 978-0-473-70276-2 (Hardback)

CONTENTS

INTRODUCTION

"Money is power, freedom, a cushion, the root of all evil, the sum of blessings."
– Carl Sandburg

Have you ever heard the cliche, "Money can't buy happiness"? It's hard to find the truth in that statement when everyone around you is racing to make as much money as possible. Whether people work two jobs to sock away money into a savings account or because they have to be able to make ends meet, the bottom line is that money is the universal language of our modern world. It's the fuel that powers dreams, the key to unlocking opportunities, and the measure of success for many. In a world where everyone seems to be in a nonstop race to grow wealth, it's crucial to recognize that the pursuit of money isn't just about accumulating it—you need to understand it, respect it, and strive to master it.

The good thing is, that the younger you are when you learn money management skills, the more financial success you can possibly reach in your life. Therefore, this book of money management tips will help you become a financial superhero in no time flat! Whether you're saving for a dream vacation, need to put yourself through college, or simply want to understand how you can make your money work for you, this book will guide you every step of the way.

Teenagers are in a strange limbo. Your parents may often still treat you like a child, checking in on you when you've been quiet for too long and ensuring you're home before curfew. However, they may also expect you to act like an adult. They want you to get a job, pick a college major, and decide what you want to do with your life—before you've even had a chance to get out there and see what the world has to offer!

By taking charge of your finances, you're putting yourself on the best path forward. You're showing the adults around you that you're taking life seriously and want to empower yourself to succeed in life. Though it may sound daunting to manage your money effectively—especially if you don't have much, *yet*—this book will walk you through all the basic knowledge you need, then go step by step through real life applications, with helpful advice on every page.

This guide isn't just about budgeting and saving, it also covers crucial topics like understanding the true value of money, how to strive for financial freedom, and different ways to earn money. There are different budgeting approaches that can benefit you in various ways, so learning how to set goals and monitor your funds will prepare you to create a strong financial safety net.

Beyond saving, investing can help your money *make* money—just by allocating funds to the stock market, mutual funds, or other smart choices. However, there are risks involved with the process, so you need to learn how to diversify your investments, meaning put them in different accounts, and do research to get the most out of the process.

You may already have some knowledge about banking and finances, but there are countless terms you should understand to ensure you're financially savvy. Do you know about taxes, loans, insurance, credit scores, inflation, and passive income? You'll learn all this and more, priming yourself to become a money guru.

You'll also learn about money minefields, those tricky situations that can trip you up and throw you off course. By knowing what to avoid, you'll set yourself on the right path to financial freedom—and this book includes tips that will ensure you're making wise choices for your future.

Each chapter covers crucial financial information that will empower you to make good choices. At the end of each chapter is an activity that reinforces what you just learned so you're ready to apply the knowledge in real life. Sometimes they're quizzes, but don't worry—they aren't for a grade! However, you want to try your best to ensure you're learning the key points to empower your financial superhero side. In some cases, the activities are actionable, asking you how you would approach a situation if you encountered it in life. Others might give you tools to help you handle your funds in real life!

In the spirit of asking questions, here are a few that give you an idea of what you'll learn in this book and prime you to think more deeply about money than just wondering what it will buy you.

1. What does financial freedom mean to you? Why is it important to you?

2. Do you currently have any money from gifts, an allowance, or a part-time job? What do you do with your money: spend, save, invest, or a little of everything?

3. What are your short-term and long-term financial goals? Do you have any idea of the steps to take to achieve them?

4. How do you imagine your financial situation in adulthood? Are there steps you can start taking as a teenager to make your dream a reality?

Did those questions make you eager to explore money in a new way? Let's not waste any time! No matter how much money experience you may or may not already have, starting with the basics is the best way to ensure we're all on the same level, so let's get started.

Chapter 1

GRASPING MONEY BASICS WITH CONFIDENCE

Whether you're starting from scratch, saving your allowance to create a solid future, or trying to find out how you can make your money work for you, this chapter will guide you through the information you need to unravel the basic principles of money, so you know what to do with it once you get your hands on some!

What Role Does Money Play in a Teen's Life?

If you're like many teens, you may not think about money because you still live at home and spend most of your time at school. You don't need much money, nor do you have much of a chance to earn it! However, learning about money as a teenager is crucial because it can provide you with a sense of independence. You can go out with friends and see a movie or have dinner without needing to borrow cash from your parents.

When you earn money from an allowance or part-time job, you're learning responsibility. You see that your time and effort are worth payment, which helps you assign a different value to money than simply how much it can buy you at a store.

As a high school student, you might not need money for your education if you're attending a public school with little to no fees, but once you graduate, you'll most likely have to pay for schooling. Whether you go to a community college, university, or trade school or take a certification course, you'll most likely have to pay for tuition, textbooks, and other fees. Scholarships and financial aid can help, but you'll need to cover some aspects yourself.

Learning about money now, while it might not make or break you, gives you the chance to understand how much you'll need in your life, for what purposes, and how you can invest and save to set yourself up for success in the future.

Do All Teens Understand the Value of Money?

Everyone is different, so it's understandable that you may not understand the value of money. It's something that many learn only when they need to, such as when they take on a part-time job or need to pay for their own gas or car insurance. Once you start getting paid a certain amount for your work or need to fork over your hard-earned cash just to get from point A to point B, you start to understand the value of money in a new way.

Many children don't think about money as they grow up. When you're young, you're lucky enough to have reliable adults and caregivers providing shelter, food, clothing, and other necessities for you. If you're really lucky, you also get toys, books, and other items that aren't necessary for a good life, but certainly make things more enjoyable. However, knowing that the coolest pair of jeans costs $50 is different than thinking of them as costing five hours of work at a fast-food restaurant! Therefore, the true value of money is something many teens don't learn until they get a job.

When you earn your own money, you start to see things in a different way.

You know that you make a certain amount of money per hour, so you better understand not only the value of money, but also the value of the goods you buy.

For example, if you make $15 an hour and want to buy a $100 pair of shoes that everyone at school is wearing, you'll have to work at least seven hours to afford them (possibly more, depending on the sales tax). However, you know from experience that trends in your school die out after a month.

Is it worth it for you to work so many hours over several days to save money for shoes that won't be cool for very long? Maybe, or maybe not. But you're thinking about it from a different point of view compared to how you used to ask your parents over and over to buy you something that was the latest trend.

Do Teens Grasp Needs vs. Wants?

The concept of your parents and guardians providing necessities begs the question: Do you understand the difference between needs and wants? Sometimes it can be tough to logically think the question through. If everyone in your school has new sneakers and you don't, you might feel like you need them to fit in and avoid being the butt of the joke for the next week. However, if you already have a durable pair of shoes, then you don't truly need anything new.

You can learn the difference between needs and wants as you start to earn money and buy your own things.

For example, you may think you need a car to get to school each day. However, when you add up the associated costs, like insurance, gas, and maintenance, you may realize that all you actually need is transportation. A bus pass for a few dollars a month may be the better deal than your own wheels.

With that in mind, you can understand how there are different levels of needs and wants. You need food to live, but it doesn't have to be a meal out with friends on a Friday night. While going out can be a blast, you'll learn how you can take that money and spend it at the grocery store, getting enough food to last you for a week! Taking a deeper look at what's behind your needs and wants can help you see things in new ways.

What Are the Essential Financial Terms a Teen Must Know?

There are many key financial terms you need to understand. This book will dive deeper into these concepts, but having a brief overview can help you know what to expect in future chapters.

- **Budget:** A plan that factors in your income and expenses to help you manage your money. You'll track where it comes from and how you spend it.

- **Compound interest:** Compound interest is like earning interest on your interest. When you save or invest money, you not only earn interest on the initial amount, but also on the interest that accumulates over time. This means your money can grow faster, especially if you start early and let it compound over many years.

- **Credit:** The ability to borrow money or access goods and services without paying anything up front, but instead promising to pay it back later. Understanding how credit works is vital to avoid debt problems.

- **Credit score:** A number used by lenders to assess how likely you are to repay loans, impacted by factors like credit, debt, and if you've repaid loans in the past.

- **Debt:** Money you owe to someone else. You can build up debt from borrowing money, and it typically comes with interest or fees.

- **Expenses:** How you spend your money, including necessities like housing, food, transportation, and other spending on items like entertainment and clothing.

- **Income:** The money you earn from a job, allowance, or other sources that you can choose to spend or save.

- **Inflation:** The gradual increase in the prices of goods and services over time, which can make it more expensive to buy things that used to be affordable.

- **Insurance:** Protection against specific risks or losses. Common types include health insurance, car insurance, and renter's insurance.

- **Interest:** You'll pay interest when you borrow money, but you can also earn it when you save money in a bank account.

- **Interest rate:** The percentage charged for borrowing money or earned on savings or investments. Higher is better when you're saving money because you earn more. But lower is better when you repay loans because you're paying back what you borrowed plus interest.

- **Investing:** Putting your money into assets like stocks, bonds, or real estate with the goal of growing your wealth over time.

- **Savings:** The portion of your income you set aside for future use or emergencies.

- **Tax:** A mandatory payment that people and businesses must pay to the government to fund public services and programs.

Can Money Change a Teen's Perspective?

Once you start to earn, spend, and save money, you'll find your perspective changes. You'll have a different approach to managing your money because you're responsible for more and want to maintain independence. As you earn money, you'll appreciate it in a different way. You know exactly how much hard work went into making each dollar you earn, so you'll value it much more.

You'll start to understand financial priorities, including setting short-term and long-term goals for saving and spending. At that point, you'll also learn to balance risk and reward when it comes to investments and spending your money.

For example, you may need to buy a car so you can get to school and work each day. However, buying a cheap used "beater" might cost you more money over time in terms of repairs, as opposed to paying off a more expensive vehicle.

Financial knowledge isn't limited to money, but also includes critical thinking and research skills.

After learning more about money, you may start to compare yourself to others. While you previously didn't notice how much money your friends have or lack, paying more attention to your financial goals may make it more clear. However, you shouldn't allow that type of comparison to discourage you or make you feel better than anyone else. Even with established savings, many are just one major emergency away from being wiped out, so be cautious and empathetic with your views. Money can create stress in many ways, and having knowledge of how to earn, invest, and handle your funds can help you feel more in control of your money and your future. With that in mind, you should feel motivated to improve your money management skills while you're still young.

Is Financial Freedom Healthy for Teens?

Financial freedom means you have enough money to pay for yourself. This is empowering for teens because it helps you accept responsibility to make wise financial decisions. It puts you on track to reach your financial goals by promoting saving, budgeting, and investing, all of which will help establish a safety net. The more knowledge you acquire as a teen, the more independent you can become in the near future. You won't have to rely on parents or guardians to spot you cash when you need something or want to go out with friends.

Financial freedom is a great way to establish confidence. When you know you have money in your wallet plus funds in the bank, you can feel like you're on your way to becoming a competent adult. This confidence will empower you to continue making wise choices.

Activity

Do you think you have a solid grasp on money basics? Answer these questions before moving on to the methods of earning money.

1. What are your current sources of income? What are your expenses?

2. What is something you'd like to buy in the future, but need to save

up for? How much money do you need to save? What associated costs might you encounter?

3. What does money mean to you? How much do you value $20 you got as a birthday gift compared to $20 you earned mowing the yard?

4. What are three things you want? What are three things you need? What is the difference between those wants and needs?

5. What role does money play in your life? What are two short-term financial goals and two long-term financial goals you have?

Chapter 2

START MAKING DOLLARS

You may think of money as numbers on paper, but when you start making dollars, you'll have that paper in your hands and see it transform into stacks of cash! Learn the secrets behind making money through allowance, babysitting gigs, and part-time jobs you can juggle on top of your already full schedule. You can even harness your creativity and become your own boss by launching an entrepreneurial venture. With the information in this chapter, you'll go from having empty pockets to filling your piggy bank with so much money that you need to deposit it at the bank. In no time, you'll be watching that bank balance grow!

Ways to Earn Money

Earning money is obviously a major step whether you plan to spend or save your funds! But how can you get started? The great thing is that there are many ways to make money these days. You can get a traditional job, like working part-time in your community or babysitting in the neighborhood. But you also have easy access to online opportunities, thanks to your phone, tablet, or computer! More and more young people are also finding success as entrepreneurs, so understanding how you can take on that venture increases your earning potential even more.

Traditional Jobs

There are many options for traditional jobs, including:

- babysitting and pet sitting

- food service

- lawn care

- lifeguarding

- retail work

For positions in food service and retail stores, you can look for listings online or visit the restaurants and stores to ask if they're hiring. You'll most likely fill out an application and get an interview if they have a spot for you. Lifeguard roles are similar, though your city government may oversee community pools and require a different application process. Many companies list open positions on their websites, so you can look online to see if they're hiring. You can also often fill out applications online.

For babysitting, pet sitting, and lawn care, you can start in your neighborhood and work from there. You may have neighbors with children or pets, so talk to them about your service for when they want a date night or are going on vacation. Establish yourself as trustworthy and then encourage them to tell others about you so you book more jobs. With those jobs and lawn care, you can make a flier to hang at local stores, libraries, and community centers. Include your contact information and services so people know what to expect when they contact you.

Online Opportunities

You can promote your babysitting, pet sitting, and lawn care services online thanks to Facebook and local sites like Nextdoor, but once you're on the internet, why not cast a wider net?

Freelancing is a great way to make money online. Do you have any of the following skills?

- graphic design

- photography

- social media management

- web development

- writing

If so, you can check out sites like Fiverr, Upwork, Freelancer, and other work platforms to connect with clients, deliver services, and get paid! With experience, you could even launch your own website and business—but you'll learn about that in the next section.

You can work online completing online surveys, as many businesses need people to conduct market research. Check out sites like Survey Junkie and Swagbucks for opportunities.

While you can leverage your social media skills to manage business accounts, you can also spend time creating content for your own outlets. You can take photos, record videos, write blogs, or record a podcast. You can earn money by monetizing your content, either by hosting ads or having sponsors.

Good students may want to tutor to earn money. You can tutor your friends and classmates in person, but when you offer your services online, you'll reach a broader audience. You can tutor students needing help with subjects you've already taken, like lower levels of math and science, or find English language learners and help them grasp grammar and conversational skills.

Entrepreneurial Ventures

Becoming an entrepreneur includes some aspects of the internet in this day and age, as mentioned above with hosting a podcast or YouTube channel, or starting a freelancing business. However, you can also sell goods as a business.

Drop-shipping and printing on demand are ways to sell products without needing to pay up front and store physical goods in your room. Use your design skills to offer artwork customers can make into shirts, notebooks, stickers, and more on sites like Printify, Redbubble, Society6, and Zazzle.

If you make items like jewelry, fiber arts, and other crafts by hand, you can start a store on Etsy. It's one of the most popular sites for homemade goods, so you can make good money by listing your crafts there.

Not everything has to be online! You can start a business for lawn care or car washing and make fliers or use word of mouth in your neighborhood and city. You can also start a business as an event planner, organizing parties and gatherings for people and companies. If you're a skilled baker or cook, you could even sell cakes and homemade treats or start a small-scale catering company.

Skills for Money-Making Success

Whether you work for a business or start your own company, there are certain skills you need for money-making success. Hard workers know their talents and understand the importance of showing up and doing their best. With money-making skills, you'll stand out as a good employee or business owner, and this will empower you to work efficiently and make more money in the process.

Some key skills include effective communication, time management, problem-solving, customer service, teamwork, and financial literacy. You most likely already have elements of these skills based on your experience in school and with friends. Transforming them to help you on the job can boost your money-making potential.

Communication Skills

Having good communication skills is essential to succeeding in your daily life, but it is especially important at work. Here are a few practical tips to help you improve your communication skills:

- **Actively listen.** This means you're showing others that you care about what they're saying.

- **Listen without interruption.** Summarize what they said to ensure you understood it correctly. This skill will help you engage with customers, colleagues, and your boss better because you'll cut down on the chances of misunderstanding.

- **Be concise.** This means to say or write things using as few words as possible to get your point across clearly and directly, without unnecessary details or explanations. The more concise you are with communication, the more professional you'll come across.

- **Hone your writing skills.** Read often and write every day, whether it's journaling, short stories, or essays, to improve your writing ability.

- **Maintain eye contact and use positive body language.** Eye contact and open, friendly gestures show that you're engaged in the conversation.

Time Management

With good time management, you'll have more time to make money. However, you may feel like you don't have the capacity to handle anything else. These tips will help you manage your time better.

- **Prioritize tasks.** Instead of wasting time procrastinating or doing a task you could outsource, use your time wisely. Always start with major tasks that will make a big impact. Once you complete those, you'll feel more productive and see how much you can do by taking action.

- **Set goals.** This inspires you to be proactive. You can set daily or weekly goals and mark them off as you complete them.

- **Divide tasks into manageable steps.** This allows you to continue making progress in small amounts. You'll always have something to do to make progress toward the big picture, so you don't waste time wondering what to do next.

- **Manage your time to stay motivated.** This can be tough if you have a lot on your plate. You'll want the satisfaction of marking things off your to-do list, so chipping away at the task will help you make progress without feeling overwhelmed.

- **Remove distractions.** Try to minimize distractions like social media while studying or working.

- **Learn to say no.** Try not to overcommit. Be aware of your limits and set boundaries to avoid overcommitting and feeling overwhelmed.

- **Take breaks.** You might think you should push through a task until it's done, but it's better to give your brain and body a break. Walk around, get some fresh air, and do something else for a few minutes before getting back to work.

Problem-Solving Abilities

Along with communication skills and time management, honing problem-solving abilities will make you a great asset to any work team. It helps you figure out solutions to problems, like puzzles in a video game, and it makes you more independent and confident. So, when you face tough situations, you'll be able to find your way through and come out stronger. Here are helpful tips:

- **Analyze situations.** Looking at all sides of an issue can prevent you from getting stuck in a problem. You can quickly assess what happened and brainstorm what to do to get out of it or fix it before it becomes a larger issue.

- **Practice regularly.** Solve puzzles, riddles, and brainteasers regularly to exercise your problem-solving muscles.

- **Think creatively.** Encourage creative thinking by brainstorming multiple solutions to a problem, even if they seem unconventional.

- **Be flexible and adaptable.** You should be open to change and willing to go with the flow,m so you don't feel stuck and experience a problem when something changes in the moment.

- **Learn from mistakes.** Embrace mistakes as learning opportunities. Analyze what went wrong and how you can approach the problem differently next time.

- **Be resourceful.** This characteristic helps you use your intelligence and what you already have to overcome any obstacle that stands in your way. It goes with flexibility and creative thinking because you're actively finding a solution based on what's around you.

- **Collaborate with others.** Work on group projects or discuss problems with friends and family to gain different perspectives and ideas.

- **Stay patient.** Problem-solving can take time, so be patient and persistent. Don't get discouraged if a solution doesn't come immediately; keep trying different approaches.

Customer Service

Customer service is a skill that may take time to develop. When you're working in food service or retail, you may have customers demanding things and treating you like you're less than them. Read on for some helpful tips on dealing with customers.

- **Listen first.** You may have a line you give to all customers in certain situations, but when you listen to the customers to understand what they need, you can then speak to them, so they know you're going to help them.

- **Handle customers well.** This is a skill that your manager and coworkers will notice. When you master this skill, your boss will appreciate how you talk to customers and give them what they want so they become repeat visitors to the business. You might even get rewarded with a bonus or raise!

- **Maintain a positive attitude.** Try to stay calm, patient, and positive, even in challenging situations. A positive attitude can go a long way in making customers feel valued and respected.

- **Utilize problem-solving skills.** You need to understand the customer's problem and have a quick, effective solution to solve it, so they feel appreciated. You don't want to lose their business, so think critically about what they need and how you can make them happy.

- **Be empathetic.** Even if a customer is being rude, you should practice empathy and active listening to understand where they're coming from. It's helpful to put yourself in the customer's shoes to better address their concerns.

Teamwork

Teamwork takes customer service a step beyond, involving collaboration, helping hands, and accountability. The following tips will help you work with others.

- **Respect differences.** You'll work with many people, from coworkers to teammates in sports to classmates you partner with for a school project. Embrace diversity within your team. People have different backgrounds, experiences, and perspectives. Respect these differences and use them to your advantage.

- **Use other skills, such as problem-solving, active listening, support, and motivation.** You may have to juggle your tasks while helping someone complete their work, which requires time management and collaboration.

- **Create a joint venture.** Say you want to start a babysitting or lawn care business, but know you can't handle all the clients alone. When you work with a team of friends, you can serve more people and make more money.

- **Pool resources.** You may want to start a photography business, but you only have a camera. Working with someone who has graphic design skills can help you set up a website, and you can offer both services to bring in more customers.

- **Network.** While you may prefer to work alone, teamwork increases your chance of networking with people who can help you later. You can make valuable connections based on who you know, which can lead to better jobs—and money-making opportunities—in the future.

Financial Literacy

Financial literacy is the information you need to make the best choices with your money. Below are tips to help you handle your money.

- **Develop financial literacy knowledge.** Financial literacy means you understand how money works and can manage it wisely.

- **Create a budget.** Once you have a budget, stick to it! You should track your expenses and income.

- **Invest your money.** Financial literacy will help you understand investment opportunities so you can grow your wealth without putting in more time and effort than necessary.

- **Avoid bad debt.** Not all debt is bad, but your knowledge will keep yours from spiraling out of control and becoming impossible to pay off. You'll know what debt you should take on.

- **Pay off the money you owe.** If you use a credit card, don't spend more each month than you can pay back without draining your bank account. Having too much outstanding debt means you'll pay more in interest. If you can't pay it back in a timely manner, you may ruin your credit score.

Benefits of Earning Money for Teens

The biggest benefit of earning money is that you have more cash to spend, right? Well, kind of. It's always fun to be able to buy a fancy coffee when you're out or get something from the mall that you've been wanting for weeks. With that in mind, you understand how having your own money is important for many reasons. However, you should also save some, and possibly invest it, to ensure you continue having your own money instead of spending each paycheck as soon as you get it. When you check out these benefits of earning money, you'll have a greater understanding of the value it adds to your life.

Gives Financial Independence

Striving for more financial independence as a teenager puts you in a great place to continue earning your own money as an adult. It can be hard to earn and save money, so when you start now, you're developing great habits that will serve you later. You can pay for yourself when you go out with friends, not needing to ask your parents to loan you money for dinner or a movie. That gives you more power over how you spend your earnings, since you won't have to give anyone a reason why you need to borrow money.

When you're financially independent, you only need to answer to yourself. So, make sure you're spending money on things you really want or need. Take time to ask yourself what you're buying and why.

Is it something you really need? It's easy to say yes to those items. Is it something you want? Think critically about why you want it. Is it a trendy clothing item that will go out of style next season? Is it something everyone at school has and you just want to fit in?

Consider your answers and think if you'd be happier with the item or with the money. Because if you don't truly want or need the item, you can save the money instead. When you start saving, you'll have a cushion in the bank for when you need money for an emergency or find something you want to buy.

Security

Speaking of having a cushion in the bank, earning money gives you security. You know you're able to do work and get paid for it, which makes you feel confident and secure in your skills. You have money when you need it and can start saving or investing to build even more wealth. Put your money in a savings account with a high interest rate so you can earn passive income every month, but still withdraw the money when you need it. If you're sure you won't need money for a certain time, you might want to consider putting it in a certificate of deposit (CD) because it will earn much more interest. Some banks offer CDs with a three-month holding period, but you can invest it for up to five years. When you withdraw the money from the CD, you'll have way more than you put in—without doing anything!

Earning your own money reduces financial stress because you don't have to worry about borrowing from people. You'll have a safety net of money, plus the potential to keep earning more through your work. Instead of stressing about filling your car with gas or taking out loans for college, you'll feel peace of mind knowing you're earning your own money to pay your way in life.

Skill Development

Working a part-time job helps you develop skills that will serve you well later in life. Even if you think you're doing an average job of ringing up customers at a fast-food place, you're still working and developing skills. You're using a cash register, interacting with the public, working together with others, and showing up for shifts. No matter what job you have, even if you only work somewhere one afternoon a week, you'll be developing skills you can later leverage to get better—and better paying—jobs.

Rewind to when you got your first job and consider the skills that the process required. The act of applying for and getting a job is already a valuable skill to have that you'll use a lot in your life, and fitting shifts into your schedule and being punctual are key time management skills you need for success in all areas of your life.

If you start an entrepreneurial venture, you'll develop even more skills than when you work for someone else. As the boss, you're going to figure out how to handle a workload, make a product, deal with customers, and process the profits. In all jobs, you'll learn about teamwork, communication, and problem-solving. You may not feel like you're developing skills when you do a task you're already familiar with, but you're learning more than you realize.

Planning for the Future

Earning money now helps you plan for the future. Even if you don't earn much at your part-time job and have to put that money toward gas or car insurance, you're already learning financial knowledge that will serve you well as you grow up. You get the chance to see how hard you work and how much money you earn for your effort. Then you pay for things you want or need and, hopefully, put some aside for the future. Even saving a small portion of your income each month can make a huge difference in terms of your future savings potential!

You'll develop forward-thinking as you earn money. You know how much work you had to do to earn a certain amount of money, so you'll look ahead and think about how you want to spend that money without feeling like you're throwing it away. You'll understand the importance of only buying things you really want or need and start saving for college, investing, moving out, a car, and other big-ticket items.

Boosts Self-Confidence

Making your own money makes you feel good! You're empowered to provide for yourself, even if you don't need to yet. When you can go out and buy your own meals, coffee, treats, or fun things, you feel good about yourself. And if you have to put that money toward bills, you feel even better because you know you're creating a good life for yourself. You can either contribute to your household and make your parents less stressed about money or pay for your own gas, car insurance, and other items your parents may take on for you, even though they shouldn't have to. Paying for yourself now will make you feel stronger about living independently and truly paying your way in life.

Having a job or running a business helps you understand how you can make a living in the future. You're already learning what you like to do and what you're good at, so you understand how to leverage these skills to make money. You're working with others to do a good job and bring home a paycheck, so you'll feel confident in your abilities and your potential to get other jobs in the future. Having a job to do and money in the bank will make you feel like a confident person.

Activity

Do you understand and appreciate the skills you have and how they can help you earn money? Answer these questions to put yourself to the test!

1. What interests or hobbies do you have? Think of five jobs that can utilize those talents, whether it's jobs you'd apply for or ways you can harness your entrepreneurial spirit and start your own business.

2. What are five ways you learned about where you can work online to earn money? Are any of these methods ways you could use to increase your earning potential?

3. What five skills are crucial for money-making success? Do you already have them, or do you need to work on developing and strengthening them?

4. How does earning money provide security in your life? How much money do you think you need to have to feel secure?

5. If you're starting to save now, what are your future plans for that money? How much money would you like to save?

Chapter 3

PLAN A SMART BUDGET

You've found a way to make money, whether you're babysitting or doing tasks around the city, working a retail job, or running your own business. So... what now? Once you have an income, you should establish a budget. This process will help you track how much money you make each month as well as how you're spending it. Your budget can include many categories for expenses, including necessary bills, fun money, and a set amount to put in your savings account or invest for future financial security.

Explore the Five Ws of Budgeting

Before you jump into budgeting, explore the five Ws to get background information. These questions will help you understand budgeting and how you can get the most out of this process. It's not about being strict and preventing yourself from buying things that make your life better. Budgeting turns into a mindset that sets you up for financial success well into adulthood, so it's best to start now.

Understanding the "Who" in Budgeting

You need to learn budgeting skills to serve you throughout your life. The more financially responsible you are, the more empowered you are to make money and have an emergency fund while still making ends meet. When you can manage your money, you give yourself independence. You won't have to scramble to find change in the couch cushions to buy a coffee when you go out after school. You'll empower yourself to buy a car and rent an apartment when you're ready without needing to stay home longer than you want or having to ask for help.

Basically, budgeting prepares you for adulthood. It helps you take responsibility for your money so you understand where it goes and can save accordingly. Ideally, budgeting helps you avoid debt. Even if you have a credit card with a high limit, you know better than to spend more than you can afford, so you don't need to borrow money or build up debt that can be tough to pay back.

The type of financial awareness you develop from budgeting will improve your financial confidence. You'll have less anxiety about money because you know how to allocate your funds to get what you need. You hone decision-making skills that help you figure out if you should buy something or save the money instead. These trade-offs can help you build your savings because you think critically before spending.

Remember that your budget is your business. You don't need to share information about your income and expenses with anyone if you don't want to or don't trust them. Your budget and money goals are personal, so don't let anyone deter you from reaching your financial dreams.

Defining the "What" in Your Budget

If you think keeping a budget seems boring or stifling, you'll love knowing there are many different approaches.

- **Static budgeting:** This is what you typically think of when it comes to budgeting. You create a fixed budget for the year based on your expected income and expenses. This gives you a clear outlook for the year, but it isn't too flexible—or interesting.

- **Flexible budgeting:** This style is ideal for teens because you can easily adapt it to your needs. Your budget reflects your real life by having a bigger entertainment budget during the summer months and more savings during the winter when you go out less with friends. However, the downside is that it takes more work to manage because you have to stay on top of your spending and track everything.

- **Envelope budgeting:** This is another quality approach for teens because it's hands-on. When you get paid, take out cash. Yes, having a savings account is great, but for this method, you want all your money in your hands. Label envelopes for each expense, such as savings, restaurants, entertainment, gas, and clothing. Put a portion of your paycheck or total money into each envelope according to what you're likely to spend. Once you use all the money in that envelope, you can't spend more in that category until your next paycheck. This method keeps you accountable and helps you see (literally) where your money is going.

If any of the outlined approaches above sound interesting, you can use it in your daily life. However, you can also find other methods, or even create one that works for you. To assess your budgeting style, start by assessing your financial goals—both long-term and short-term. You'll want to add categories for what you need to save, so you'll have that covered.

Take an honest look at your income and expenses. If you don't make much money because you work part-time, it's unrealistic to plan to travel the world in the next two months because you can't set aside enough savings. But this honesty helps, because you'll see your goals and strive to meet them, so it's easier to curb unnecessary spending.

You can always start with one budgeting method and see how it works for you. If you find that you're not saving enough and keep pulling money from other categories, reassess your approach. Ensure you're breaking your goals into attainable steps and giving yourself enough time to reach them.

For example, you can start saving for that trip around the world now and aim to make it a reality within two years. Having that deadline can make you feel more purposeful with budgeting.

Timing Matters: "When" to Create and Review Your Budget

Finances change and you might find new goals to reach. You might have unexpected expenses or get a car as a gift and need to put money aside for gas and insurance. Your life isn't static, so your budget shouldn't be fixed either.

The more you look at your budget, the more you're thinking about your financial situation, which can boost your savings potential. Maybe you look at your budget after two months and realize you haven't spent any money at restaurants, so you can put that into savings and change the category going forward.

Reviewing your budget will show your spending patterns and help you assess your needs and wants. Maybe you've kept receipts that show you're spending too much money on clothing.

Think about how often and why you buy clothes. Do you wear them enough to make it worth the expense? Try to reduce your clothing budget for a month or two and see how it affects you.

Regular budget reviews will help you adapt to changes in your life and prevent overspending, which can really throw you off track for your long-term goals.

Allocating Resources: "Where" Your Money Goes

The biggest appeal of a budget is being able to see where your money goes. If you find yourself short on bills or pulling from savings each month, you'll understand that you need to review your budget and make some changes.

Start by reviewing the necessities, including bills and expenses, that are essential for your daily life. For now, those necessities might only include your cell phone bill, car insurance, and gas, but learning how to allocate your money now will help you in the future when your essentials include housing, groceries, utilities, and healthcare. Write down your recurring monthly expenses to see where that money goes. Then, you can take steps to cut corners within these categories, like finding a more affordable cell phone provider or being more efficient with your errands so you use less gas.

You should also allocate money for savings. Ensuring you can put money away each month will give you a buffer when you hit unexpected expenses. You can pull money from your emergency fund if you're short on income one month. You can also save money toward short-term goals, like buying a new laptop or scoring concert tickets.

Your spending will also include a discretionary fund, which is fun money. This is another area where you can cut corners if you're unable to pay your other bills. Discretionary funds can include money you spend on movies, restaurants, games, hobbies, shopping, and travel. Write down where everything goes so you can understand your spending habits.

Discovering the "Why" Behind Your Budget

A smart budget means you're prioritizing your financial stability while still buying the things you need without being wasteful. You can create a smart budget by setting goals, like paying for college, buying a car, or going on vacation. When you have a goal in mind, you can create a detailed approach to how you'll save that money.

Include all income, like paychecks from a job and allowance from your parents. Then, write down everything you spend on each month, whether it's for school lunches, nights out with friends, gas for your car, or other costs. When you live independently, these costs will include your rent, groceries, utilities, and other big bills.

Always include space for savings, but be realistic. You want a smart budget, not something unattainable that makes you feel bad when you fall short.

For example, don't say you're going to save $200 a month when you only make $300 from your part-time job and have to pay for gas, nights out with friends, or new clothes.

Prioritize saving money and only spending what you need to spend, but also be flexible with yourself. Know that some months you might encounter unexpected expenses and be unable to save at all, and just roll with it when that happens. You'll already have the smart budget mindset, so you can stay on this savings path without feeling like you've lost your goal.

Strategies to Plan a Smart Budget

Planning a smart budget takes work. Even if you have a good idea of how much money you make compared to what you spend, putting it on paper (or in an app!) might help you see things differently. Money can be abstract for some people, especially if your job pays via direct deposit and you spend money with a debit or credit card. When you don't hold the money and see it leaving your hands, it's harder to grasp how much you're actually making and spending.

Check Your Earnings

Before you can budget your money, you need to know how much you have coming in. Your earnings include any income you make on a semi-regular basis, so you can factor it into your budget.

For example, if you work at a store in the mall after school and babysit every weekend, you can calculate those earnings into your budget. However, if you only earn money when you mow the grass at home, you'll have a harder time establishing a budget you can stick to, since you won't have a set mowing schedule throughout the year.

Therefore, the information in the previous chapter about finding a job is crucial! You want to find something that provides a regular paycheck, without taxing yourself too much when it comes to juggling school and your other responsibilities.

Even if you have a job, your hours might vary week by week. You might need to take time off for a school event or travel to a competition with the band or a team. When you don't work a set schedule, your pay can vary each month. However, you can still estimate your income for budgeting purposes, and fill in the exact amounts once you get your paychecks for the month.

Plan Your Essential Expenses

The key to a quality budget is to pay all your necessary expenses first. If you have to pay for gas and car insurance, those come out of your income before anything else. If you live independently, you need to prioritize rent, insurance, utilities, and groceries above all. Essential expenses are ones you'd most likely have every month. Even if you pay car insurance every six months, you can add it into your monthly budget to ensure you have the money when you need it.

One great way to understand budgeting is the "50-30-20" rule. This means you spend 50% of your income on things you need, 30% on things you want, and 20% on savings. How you break down that 30% for wants is up to you. Let's check out an example.

If you make $1,000 a month, that means $500 goes toward your expenses, like food, car insurance, gas, and school needs. You can spend $300 on whatever you want, which may mean you allocate $100 for going out with friends, $100 for video games, and $100 for fast food. Maybe you want to spend $150 for date nights, $50 on gourmet coffee, and $100 on decor for your room. This category is the one that has the most flexibility, because you know that $500 is for needs and $200 is for savings.

Define Your Expenditure Limits

Your limits need to fall within how much money you earn, of course, but beyond that, you have a lot of flexibility with each category you create. Once you set aside money for your essential expenses, you might choose categories such as:

- clothing and accessories

- entertainment with friends

- games, music, and movies

- restaurants

- savings

You can also create more general classifications, like "wants" and "savings." You can put a portion of your income into savings and then spend the rest however you see fit, whether it's buying the latest video game or going to a pizza place with your friends every Friday. Even though you're not budgeting for every item, you're still sticking to a broad spending limit that will help you save money.

Set Your Saving Goals

While your budget will help you see where you spend money, you should also set some aside for savings. Start by determining a goal for your savings account. It can be a concrete goal, like having $1,000 by the end of the year or having a down payment for a car before your next birthday. It can also be more abstract, like just trying to save money so you'll have a security net if you need it. You can even set up savings accounts for different purposes, like a general savings account and another for your goal.

Track your savings on your budget just as you track expenses. You want to see how much you put aside each month, whether it's always $50 or a percentage of your income that may vary over time.

Allot Money for Emergency Funds

Regardless of your specific savings goals, an emergency fund is a smart choice. When you add this item to your budget, you're guaranteeing yourself a safety net in case something unexpected happens. Maybe you need to buy special supplies for a school project at the last minute or have to pay for car repairs. Knowing that you have money set aside for that type of occurrence can alleviate a lot of stress. This account is one you can keep adding to and let the interest rate add more money monthly so you always have funds on hand, no matter what your monthly budget may look like.

Use Budgeting Apps

Keeping a paper budget might be boring. Maybe you're not a spreadsheet person, either. Thankfully there are budgeting apps that are easy to use. Best of all, they're convenient! You can track your spending while you're on the go, instead of forgetting what you bought by the time you make it home after a long day. Look into these apps to see how they can help:

- Expensify

- Goodbudget

- Mint

- PocketGuard

- You Need a Budget (YNAB)

As an active teen, you already have a lot going on in your life. Budgeting might seem like another task you have to make time for, so you put it off.

However, financial security is so important that you really should prioritize budgeting. Therefore, linking a budgeting app to your bank account and credit card will immediately track data without you having to do any of the work yourself.

Leave Scope for Adjustments

Even with a thoughtful budget, you're still going to have some adjustments each month. Perhaps you had to deal with an unexpected car repair before you had enough money in your emergency fund to cover it. Or you had to buy birthday or holiday gifts for your loved one and forgot to add it to the budget.

Being able to adjust your budget each month will empower you to take even more control over your expenses and savings. Instead of blindly following the same guidelines, you're actively assessing your budget and changing it when necessary.

Plan Your Budget Every Month

Some people make annual budgets to ensure they stay on track for long-term goals, but it's best if you plan your budget every month. This will get you in the habit of thinking about your money more often than at the beginning and end of the year. When you make a monthly budget, you can look at your schedule and plan accordingly. Maybe you need to buy a birthday gift for your best friend or budget money for a date night. You might need to put more into savings because you don't have extra expenses this month and want to cushion your emergency fund.

Planning your budget each month also gives you a chance to look back over your spending. You can see what you spent and saved last month to get a better understanding of your habits. Regularly checking on this type of information can help you adapt your mindset for a stronger financial approach moving forward.

Benefits of Budgeting for Teens

Budgeting is important because it helps you manage your money, even if you don't have much. The act of creating a budget requires critical thinking, and sticking to it is even more impressive! Making and maintaining a budget can reduce the stress and anxiety you feel when it comes to needing to pay for your own things or save up for big purchases, so it's a great skill to practice as you get older.

Helps Manage Finances

When you have a budget, you can see how much money you bring in and where it goes. Whether you have a job, get an allowance, or get money as gifts, your income is important and you want to spend wisely. Making a budget ahead of time helps you see how much money you need each month for your bills or fun outings with friends. Checking over your expenses at the end of each month will show you what you actually spent and where that money went.

For example, if you end up spending more on meals out with friends, you can decide to increase that budget category the next month. If you need to save more, you can get stricter with yourself when you go out. You wouldn't have any of this information without a budget, though, so it truly helps manage finances.

Makes Scope for Savings

If you get money and spend it before it even hits your wallet, you're unable to save anything. Creating a budget gives you a chance to look at your income and expenses and tell yourself how much you can spend on each category, including putting money into savings.

A savings account is important because you might want to save up for something big, like a car or your first apartment. You might need to save money for college tuition. You and your friends may plan to take fun trips or go to concerts, and your savings account can cover those expenses. Even if you don't have something in mind to save up for, creating an emergency account will give you financial protection in the future.

Reduces Money-Related Stress

That emergency fund will reduce money-related stress, but so does budgeting in general. When you track how much money you make and spend, you won't feel anxious wondering if you have enough to cover certain bills or fun events each month. You'll have already calculated a budget that gives you money for each important expense in your life.

You may not be rolling in dough, but budgeting whatever money you have can reduce stress because you remain totally in control. You know exactly how much money you have and can tell yourself what to spend it on and how much to save, which gives you a sense of power over your life that will reduce stress and anxiety.

Establishes Good Money Habits

Budgeting puts you in the mindset of creating and following good money habits. When you start budgeting the money you make from an allowance or part-time job, you're teaching yourself how to take care of your needs financially. This skill will serve you well as you grow up and position you to become an adult who's in control of their money and can live a financially comfortable life.

You're already learning how to consider every dollar you earn, spending it carefully on things you want and need. You'll also understand the importance of tracking your spending, which serves you well once you open a credit card. You'll already know how to check your expenses, so you're less likely to get a surprise credit card bill with a massive outstanding balance.

Budgeting is a skill you'll develop over time, so starting now empowers you to save money and spend thoughtfully. It involves tracking your income and expenses, so you always know how much money you bring in and how you're spending it. This practice helps you make thoughtful spending decisions and teaches you how to prioritize savings. Over time, you'll develop financial discipline and responsibility, setting you up for success as you reach adulthood and bring in a larger income.

Activity

Before you create a budget, you need to track your expenses. Save your receipts for three months or track your spending through your online bank account or credit card statement to fill out this worksheet. Three months will give you a chance to notice a pattern in your spending. It also gives you some leeway, like if you spend a lot in December because you're buying gifts for others, but don't spend as much in November and January.

Expense	Month 1	Month 2	Month 3	Total Spent
Fast food				
Coffee				
Video games				
Cell phone				
Streaming services				
Car insurance				
Gas				
Gifts for others				
School supplies				
Clothing				

There are suggestions filled in along with space to write in your other purchases. Be honest with yourself here, as this will help you budget. You may notice that you spend a lot of money buying random tech, like earbuds or webcams. You might go to a store and buy makeup or random items just to have something to do. Write down every expense so you can make a realistic budget for yourself.

Once you fill in the worksheet, highlight the name of the necessary expenses. Look at how much you spent over the past three months and see if there's a pattern. Maybe you spend $100 a month on coffee that could be saved by brewing cups at home. Maybe you go out to eat with friends even if you've already had dinner at home, just to be social, but you end up buying a meal you don't eat. Make notes on what you're spending and think critically about why you spend this money.

Use this worksheet to create your budget. First, budget your money for your highlighted necessary expenses. Then look at where else your money goes and consider how you can lower the amount spent to put more into your savings account. This will help you create a budget.

Make copies of this worksheet to use periodically. It's great to reassess your budget every few months to ensure you're staying on track with your savings and spending.

Chapter 4

KNOW THE TRICKS TO INVEST MONEY

You might think you're too young to start investing money, but the earlier you start, the more you increase your earning potential. When it comes to investments, you can choose high- or low-risk options. With high-risk investments, you might make a lot of money very quickly, but you can also lose money. For low-risk investments, you can invest money now and leave it for over 30 years or until retirement, giving it time to grow slowly but surely. However, before you start investing, you need to understand the b asics.

You can invest in stocks, bonds, mutual funds, CDs, and even real estate. Each option has pros and cons that can help you protect and grow your money. When you consider each of these options, you need to think of your goals. Are you trying to save a lot of money in just a few years to pay your college tuition? Do you want to buy a house by the time you turn 30, giving your money 12 to 15 years to grow? Or are you saving for retirement and can easily put money away for 50 years to create a massive nest egg to live off in the future? Goals impact the type of investment you should choose, so read on to learn what you need to know to make your money work for you.

What Is Investing?

Investing sounds intimidating to many people because your money may seem locked away. If you invest in real estate or a CD, you can't dip into them when you need a little extra money like you could withdraw from your savings account. But you should also consider that, when invested properly, your money has great potential to grow. While you can't readily access it, you're going to have a bigger nest egg the longer you let it sit, so it's worth having patience to achieve financial success.

The Power of Compound Interest

Compound interest feels like magic because your money grows without you needing to do anything at all. When you picture yourself making money, you probably see yourself at work, earning $15 or so per hour. After two hours, your money is now $30; after a four-hour shift, you have $60. Your money is growing, but you're working hard for it. With compound interest, you don't have to do the work.

Let's say you invest $100 in a bank account that has an annual interest rate of 5%. At the end of the first year, you'll earn 5% of $100, bringing your account total up to $105. That means, going into the second year of the account, it's like you've invested $105, and the 5% interest is on top of that amount instead of your initial investment. So, by the end of the second year, you'll have earned $5.25 in interest, bringing your new bank balance up to $110.25. In two years, you'll have made $10.25 without doing anything.

That amount may seem small, but remember that some accounts have different interest rates, and the more you invest, the more you'll make. Compound interest should inspire you to put more money toward savings instead of spending it on coffee and meals out with friends, because you'll continue earning more and more.

Why Should Teens Start Investing Early?

You should start investing early because it's a long-term game, so starting now gives you even more time to let your money grow. The market will naturally have ups and downs, so the longer you can leave your money alone, the more likely you'll make more from the interest and investments. Retirement may seem far away, but the years will fly by. As you're busy living your best life, your investment accounts will be growing to provide you with a financially secure future in your golden years.

Investing now helps you build good habits because you're learning to save and be smart with your money. You can also see investing as a learning opportunity because you'll keep an eye on the market and learn how it can rise and fall, and what issues make that happen! You'll start making informed decisions based on critical thinking and processing information from multiple sources, focused on your financial health.

By investing now, you're setting yourself up for financial independence. You can make smart choices that make it easy for you to buy a new car, pay your college tuition, or move out of your parent's home into your own apartment. Making the most of these life landmarks means you need to have financial knowledge, and investments can help you get there.

Interesting Ways to Invest Money for Teens

Investing money is a smart way to become financially secure. However, investing may seem boring and complex. Once you look into all the different options, you'll see that there are many exciting ways to invest money and maximize your earning potential. Based on your goals and interests, you can decide to play it safe with a savings account or ride the roller coaster of the stock market.

Stock Market

The stock market may seem like it has the highest highs and the lowest lows, but that's just what you hear about in the news. Starting in the stock market is a great way to invest your money and grow wealth. The stock market gives you the chance to buy shares of ownership in companies. The companies use the money from selling stock to pay for their business. If the company does well, the value of the stock increases and you can sell it for more than you initially paid.

The stock market is a great way to build wealth over time. If you can invest money in a company and leave it, you're more likely to earn money as the company grows. You should know about the risks and market trends, though, which means you may not make your money back and have to sell at a loss.

You can research stock exchanges like the New York Stock Exchange (NYSE) and Nasdaq. Companies list their shares on these outlets so you can buy shares through a brokerage account. When you buy a share of stock, you now have ownership in that company and can benefit from its earnings. The price of a stock can change daily and with demand, so you should research when to buy a stock before the price goes up because everyone wants it. Websites like Fidelity, Charles Schwab, and Ameritrade can help you get started with research and investing.

If you're interested in investing in the stock market, but you're under 18, you can talk to your parents or guardians and open a custodial brokerage account. Together with the adult, you can jointly manage the account until you're 18 and take full control.

Bonds and Fixed-Income Investments

Stocks are one of the most commonly known investments, but bonds and fixed-income investments are also great choices for teens. Basically, bonds are loans you give to a company or the government. You buy a bond, giving them your money to use as they see fit. They promise to pay you back at a certain date, giving you the original amount you paid plus interest payments in the meantime. The interest payments are a percentage of the bond's face value.

Bonds aren't as risky as the stock market. Because you're loaning money to a company or the government, you're guaranteed to get your money back plus interest, so there's no need to expect the rise and fall of value like the stock market. While you're waiting to reach the bond's maturity date, you'll get coupon payments of interest, so you'll get passive income during your wait.

You may think bonds seem boring compared to the exciting potential of the stock market, but the best part is that you can invest in both! Diversification basically means you're not putting all your eggs in one basket. Instead of investing $1,000 in the stock market, you can invest $500 there and $500 in bonds, increasing your earning potential and giving you more chances to invest. These accounts make up your portfolio, which is a fancy word meaning the collection of your investments.

Mutual Funds

Mutual funds are investments that pool money from many investors to buy various assets, including stocks and bonds, so you have money working for you in different ways. You don't need to actively track your investment as much because a professional fund manager oversees things, making the best investment decisions for everyone involved. Since you buy shares of the fund with others, you don't need to give as much money to get many different investment options.

Instead of needing to learn about various investment options, mutual funds are ideal for teens because your money will go toward many assets for the best diversification. It reduces the risk of poor-performing investments because you have so many active options. There's a professional manager, so you can kick back and let your money work for you without needing to monitor the stock market and check the value of your investment daily. Also, since you're pooling resources with other investors, it's one of the most affordable options. If you need that money quickly, you can buy or sell shares because your investment stays relatively liquid compared to other options. You can also continually invest more money in mutual funds to increase your investment payout.

Exchange-Traded Funds

Exchange-traded funds (ETFs) are investments in the stock market, but they're more diverse than buying a single company's stock, so you can greatly increase your earning potential. You can choose a specific group, like bonds, commodities, or stocks, and see financial growth from several sources.

For example, you can invest in a stock ETF that owns stock in many different companies across industries.

Yes, you're investing in the stock market only, but you're going to get a lot of options with that one investment, which can pay off. They're also lower cost compared to managed mutual funds, so more of your money goes directly to the stock instead of the manager.

Like mutual funds, ETFs offer liquidity, meaning you can sell shares during the trading day if you need to access money. You don't have to worry about your money getting tied up in the stock and being unable to pay your bills. Even though you've invested a certain amount in ETFs, you can sell shares to get the money in cash instead of having to wait a set period of time to access it.

You can invest in an ETF now by opening an investment account; get help from a guardian if you're under 18. You can choose an ETF based on your financial goals and how much risk you're willing to take with your money. When you regularly contribute even small amounts of money, you'll see a significant increase in your funds.

Savings Accounts

Savings accounts are the safest investment opportunity because your money stays in the bank, and the Federal Deposit Insurance Corporation (FDIC) insures your money up to a certain limit. This means that the bank can run into trouble and you'll still have your full amount of money insured, so you won't go broke just because the bank closes down. It's easy to open a savings account at any bank near you, and you can withdraw cash whenever you need it.

With that in mind, you can easily open a savings account for emergency funds, college tuition, a car, or any other goal you have in mind. In most cases, you'll need to have a government-issued ID and Social Security number. If you're under 18, you'll need a parent or guardian to cosign with you, just as you need them for other investment options.

A savings account helps you earn money due to its interest rate. Some banks have low interest rates, so shop around for one that will pay off in time. You can deposit money regularly and see your savings grow due to the modest interest rate.

If you need to improve your financial literacy, starting with a savings account as an investment option is the best way to go. You'll learn about deposits, withdrawals, interest, and savings. You can track your account online or via an app so you can easily integrate a savings account into your budgeting approach.

Certificates of Deposit

CDs are special savings accounts banks offer, so they're also insured by the FDIC. They have a specific time limit and a higher interest rate than a standard savings account. The catch is that you must keep your money in the CD until the time is up, or else you'll have to pay a penalty.

For example, you can put $500 in a CD for one year and get an interest rate that may be double what the bank offers on standard savings accounts. At the end of the term, you may withdraw $750 or more depending on the interest rate, but you can't withdraw any money before the end of the term.

CDs are good investment options for teens because they're safe and payout in a big way. There's no risk of losing your investment like there is with the stock market. You'll also learn a lot about interest by investing in CDs. You'll develop discipline by being unable to access that investment, so it can really help you change your financial habits.

Visit your bank and ask what CDs they offer. You can choose the terms based on how much money you want to earn or how long you can keep that money tied up. Once the CD term ends, you can withdraw the money without consequence. You can also decide to renew the CD and continue earning more money from your initial investment.

Real Estate Investing

Real estate investing can be tough for teens to break into since it requires a substantial up-front investment, but learning about it now can help you make good choices in the future.

For example, you may have the goal of saving enough money now to buy a house near campus by the time you enroll in college. You can live there until graduation, then rent it out to other students to make money while you move elsewhere.

Real estate investments are when you buy property to generate income. You can do this either by purchasing a property, like a house or apartment to rent, or investing in real estate investment trusts (REITs). REITs are companies that finance income-generating real estate, so you can make money by being a part of their company.

Real estate is one of the best ways to build long-term wealth because most property values increase over time, and people always need a place to live, so you're basically guaranteed potential income with property in a way you're not with the stock market. You can generate consistent passive income by renting out a property.

As a teenager, you'll want to research REITs to get a taste of real estate investments. You can understand the real estate market without needing enough money to buy a house on your own. There are many types of REITs, including residential, commercial, and retail, so you can invest in different property classifications. Commercial real estate includes any property used for business purposes instead of living spaces. Retail real estate includes buildings and properties for stores, shopping centers, and malls. Generating income through an REIT can help you grow wealth and make you excited to invest in real estate more once you've earned enough money.

There are plenty of ways to invest your money, and all have benefits and risks. Consider your financial goals and how much you can invest now before making a choice. Research is key and talk to your parents or guardians about what they're willing to help you with when it comes to cosigning and custodial accounts, which give you access to their accounts and credit cards so you can learn how to manage money with less risk to your credit and finances.

Factors to Consider for Teen Investors

Learning about the various investment opportunities is just the tip of the iceberg. You want to grow your wealth, but you need to understand exactly what you're getting into. There are risks involved with any investment, so you need to think about how much money you're willing to lose for the chance to earn more than you can imagine. Being open with yourself about your options will help you make informed decisions regarding investments.

Risk Tolerance

Before you invest a penny, you need to consider your risk tolerance. When you invest $100 in the stock market, you could watch it grow to $1,000 or see it dwindle away so that you lose money on your investment. You need to think about how willing you are to see your money fluctuate. It can be tough to see your hard-earned cash make several hundred dollars and then lose it all for no reason you can understand. You also need to consider your ability to lose this money. If you have no savings and need money to pay bills, it's better you keep your $100 instead of investing it, since you might lose it all.

Since you're planning to start investing as a teenager, you can take on more risk. You have decades before you'll need some of this money in the case of retirement investing, so you don't need to worry about losing a lot of money right now since you won't need it until later. You could even invest money in various stocks and accounts that are a mix of high and low risk, to ensure you have investments ready for the near future and for your retirement.

Time Horizon

As you might realize from reading about risk tolerance, your timeline can make a huge difference in your investment approach. Since you're starting young, you have more time to allow money to grow at a slower pace. The market fluctuations won't affect you as much because even a major loss still has time to grow and give you a great payout. Market fluctuations can happen based on politics, the economy, or other aspects that impact daily life and the value of money. That can mean the value of your accounts changes drastically day to day, but will even out over time.

People who don't invest until they're older don't have that much time. If someone is 50 and wants to create a retirement account, they may only have 15 years to get enough money to live off of when they quit work. They'll need to take on more risk by choosing stocks that can deliver more possible income in a shorter amount of time. Since you have 50 or more years before retirement, you can invest less money in lower-risk accounts and see more of a payout than the 50-year-old investor ever will.

However, you also need to consider your time horizon when it comes to each goal. Saving for retirement is one thing, but you may need to save to pay college tuition in the next few years. You may also simply need to start a savings account for an emergency fund of money you can access at any time. Consider all aspects of your goals and timelines to ensure you invest cautiously and can provide for whatever you need.

Diversification

Learning about all the investment options hopefully grabbed your interest.

Even if only one investment option sounded interesting, you should consider diversification. In most cases, it pays off to have money in multiple investments because you'll continually earn more compared to keeping your money in a low-interest account.

When you diversify your investments, you spread the risk of losing your money and tanking your earning potential. If the stock market takes a nosedive, you may not lose all your money because your bonds and ETFs can still hold steady.

As a teenager, you want to explore all of your options. Even if stocks seem to have the most potential, you should also try bonds, ETFs, and REITs. You're young, so you have time to make back any money you may lose in an investment approach that's not right for you. However, you might realize that something that seemed boring at first is actually a major payday. Try all your options before deciding you want to stick with one or two investment opportunities—you may be surprised at the outcome.

Research and Due Diligence

This section might have made you excited to make passive income, which means you can generate money without working, like through the stock market and compound interest. Hopefully it also showed you how important it is to research before taking action. You may think it's simple to create a brokerage account and start investing, but you need to understand what you're getting into. Research stocks, bonds, mutual funds, and other assets before you hand over a penny of your own money. You need to understand what a company does and how likely they are to make a profit. Even if you plan to give a fund manager complete control of your money, you want to have some basic knowledge about what you're doing for risk assessment, if nothing else.

Check financial news websites and investment books for information on this process. You can also talk to your parents or trusted financial advisors to get personalized advice on investing for your specific goals.

Investing as a teenager is a major step forward, not only putting you on the right path toward financial independence, but also giving you a leg up for wealth-building. When you take your foundational knowledge and consider risk tolerance and your timeline, you're preparing yourself to make informed decisions that will help you achieve your financial goals.

Simple Steps to Start Investing for Teens

Learning about the types of investment opportunities gives you a broad overview of how you can get started in this field. However, you should take a deeper dive to ensure you know what steps you need to take to invest your money in the smartest way possible. By following these steps, you can start on your journey of financial empowerment. Your investments will build a solid foundation for your future financial success.

Step 1. Explore and Learn About Investing Options

The first step toward investing is to explore, learn, and conduct research. This chapter is a great way to get started learning, but it's mostly general information to serve as your launchpad. You'll want to get more specific in your research by looking deeper into stocks, bonds, mutual funds, ETFs, REITs, and other investment opportunities. There are risks and rewards associated with each option, so you'll want to take notes and then assess which align best with your financial goals and overall approach to money.

While it's ideal to start investing as soon as you can, that simply refers to starting now, when you're a teenager and have your whole life ahead of you. That doesn't mean you need to skip taking a few weeks to research before you hand over your hard-earned money. Look online for resources, books, and courses tailored toward teen and newbie investors. This information will be more accessible because you won't need extensive financial knowledge, and will be more approachable because it won't require that you have thousands of dollars ready to invest.

Step 2. Set Clear Investment Goals

Before handing over money, you should understand your investment goals and know that your approach will help you reach them.

For example, if you're 16 and need to save money to pay for college, putting your part-time paycheck in a savings account won't help you earn as much money as you'll need in the near future. With that goal and timeline, it's better to look at a CD with a high interest rate and invest your money for two years to see it grow.

You might not have a fixed goal for your investment. People saving for retirement will have a deadline in place, but may not have a specific financial goal they need to reach. Similarly, if you're mostly saving to establish an emergency fund, you may have a broad goal of earning as much as you can. There's no need to pressure yourself to put a dollar amount on that type of goal, as long as you trust yourself to prioritize savings when it comes to making and tracking your budget.

When you do have specific goals, keep them in mind as you determine your investment strategy. Make notes of your timeline and goal savings amount to assess how much of a risk you're willing to take and narrow down your investment options.

Step 3. Create a Portfolio

Creating a portfolio will help you collect and oversee your investments. A portfolio is like a collection of different financial investments. You can regularly monitor your portfolio and make changes as necessary to ensure you're on track to meet your goals. Remember that the market fluctuates often, so you should keep a level head if you check in and see that you lost money one day. Know it will balance out in time and keep monitoring it to ensure the company's stock isn't plummeting for good reason.

Ideally, you diversify your investments so much that you always have your money working for you. This means you want to see everything, even when you have different asset classes, like stocks, bonds, and real estate. You can also diversify your portfolio by industry.

For example, you can buy stocks in retail companies, engineering companies, and software manufacturers. While you still have a set amount of money invested in stocks, you're going to make money in different industries that have diverse risks and payoffs.

This process can help increase your potential to earn stable returns.

Step 4. Regular Check-Ins

Investing isn't like putting money in a savings account and letting it sit. You need to check in frequently to ensure they're paying off and keeping you on track for your financial goals. You can always adjust your investments, so the more you check in, the quicker you can decide if something isn't working, pull your money, and invest in another avenue.

Over time, your risk tolerance may change and you'll need to adjust your investment strategy. This may also happen when your timeline changes. The more you assess your portfolio, the better equipped you are to maintain your earning potential.

Step 5. Stay Informed

Finances are never stagnant. The stock market fluctuates every day and is greatly impacted by things happening in the country and around the world. You want to stay informed so you can determine how certain things may impact your investments. You should read up on market trends, economic developments, and investment news. The more you know, the better informed you are when making investment decisions.

You can set up Google Alerts for the stock market or specific investment opportunities. You can also join online forums where other investors talk about their ideas and strategies. Even if you only read and don't post or participate, you're taking in their knowledge and using it for your benefit.

Investing is a way to make your money work for you. Compound interest and the stock market are ways to let your accounts earn money while you live your life. Starting early gives you the most time to ensure your money can grow, even if you only invest a small amount to start. With the promise of long-term rewards, your investing journey can have a major payoff that sets you up for financial success.

Activity

Practice online investing—without putting your money at risk. This is a practice activity that will help you develop real-life skills.

Research stocks online and think of what companies you'd want to support. You should consider many aspects of the company, including if they align with your values and if they have money-making potential. While you want to support organizations that matter to you, you also need to be smart and choose ones that are more likely to be successful because that means they'll grow your money the most.

Pretend you have $1,000 to invest. Choose a few companies to invest in, with the goal of "buying" 10 shares of each. This means you'll have to budget your initial $1,000 investment carefully! Ask yourself if it's better to buy 10 shares of one high-performing company or 10 shares of several decent-performing companies.

When you select your stocks, write down the date and purchase price in the worksheet below. Consider how much money you have to invest and how many shares that will buy. For example, if a stock is $2, you can buy 100 shares for $200. After a month, record the stock's value and then calculate how much money you've earned or lost.

Date	Stock	Share Price	Money Available to Invest	# of Shares Bought	Date	New Share Price	Amount Earned or Lost

Chapter 5

LEARN THE ART OF SAVING MONEY

Saving money truly is an art—it's something you need to practice and hone over time until you become a master. As soon as you start earning money, whether it's an allowance or from a job, you can start creating the foundation of good habits that empower you to save money. When you save, you have a safety net that can protect you in case of financial emergencies. You'll have the skills needed to learn how to achieve your financial goals and become fully independent.

Importance of Saving Money for Teens

Smartphones, tablets, and access to the internet at all times has made instant gratification the standard for most things. Instant gratification means you get what you want or need as soon as you seek it.

For example, you can look up the answer to a question, listen to music, and contact friends in just a few seconds with your phone at your fingertips. However, saving money isn't that simple. It takes time to earn and save money and patience to watch your bank account grow.

While your goal for saving money may be to establish a nest egg for college or buy your first home, that isn't all you're doing with this process. You're creating strong habits that help you become a responsible person because you're saving money instead of spending it as soon as you earn it.

Acts as a Building Block for Financial Independence

Saving money acts as a building block for financial independence. In fact, you could argue that it's the foundation of independence. When you save money, you're giving yourself resources you'll need when you live on your own. Earning money gives you a different interpretation of the value of each dollar. Accumulating hard-earned money helps you feel in control and gives you the chance to make wise choices with your money in terms of how you spend or save it.

When you start working, you need to set some financial goals. Think of things you'd like to save up to buy along with how much money you'd like to have in your savings account for emergencies or anything else. Your financial goals can also include more general terms, like how much you're willing to spend on fun things each month compared to how much you deposit into savings.

You'll feel a sense of accomplishment when you save money, regardless of how you plan to spend those funds. You'll continually reach new milestones in your savings journey, allowing you to save a certain benchmark amount and invest in the big-ticket items you set a goal to purchase.

Gives the Control of Money in the Hands of Teens

Learning how to save money gives you control of your money, which leads you to financial independence. You won't have to rely on your parents to loan you money to buy things you want. You won't find yourself out with friends, unable to join them for dinner because you don't have your own money and don't want to ask one of them to cover your bill. Financial independence helps you feel confident and mature because you're able to fund your life.

The more you save, the more you'll learn about money management. You're already learning about budgeting and investment opportunities just from reading this book. When you have money in your account, you'll learn even more about interest rates, investments, and passive income. You'll have a chance to get a credit card and establish a strong credit score that will help you secure loans, property, and cars in adulthood. Financial knowledge can also protect you from falling for scams that drain your bank accounts, which will reduce your stress levels and empower you to be more proactive when making money decisions.

Independence is one thing you'll learn from saving money, but financial security is also a major perk. You don't have to set long-term goals to have a reason to save; you can save because you want to know you have money in the bank when you need it. The more you save, the less likely you are to impulsively spend your money, buying things you don't really need.

Some Tips to Help You Save Money

It can be tough to prioritize saving money when there's so much out there calling your name. You may want the latest phone or to splurge on concert tickets for your favorite band. You may like buying the newest fashions, so you fit in with your friends at school. You and your friends might go out every weekend, grabbing coffee, having dinner, or seeing movies together. It's understandable that you want to feel like you're part of something, whether it's a new trend or your social circle. But you don't always have to spend money to fit in, so these tips will help you prioritize saving money.

Developing a Saving Mindset

The most helpful tip for money management is to develop a saving mindset. Once you rewire your brain to prioritize saving money over spending it, then it's easier than ever to grow your bank balance. This step requires you to recognize the value of money in terms of how you earned it and what it could buy you. Instead of dropping $50 on a new shirt, think about how hard you worked to earn that money and how it could pay your phone bill or a portion of your car insurance instead. You'll start to understand that practical spending is best. After you pay your necessary expenses, you'll feel more inclined to save the rest of your money instead of spending it on something fun but temporary, like fleeting fashion or a single meal out with friends.

Setting goals can help you develop a saving mindset. When you know you're saving up for specific things, it's easier to put money away because you'll feel motivated to make progress. As you spend money, track the expenses so you know where your money goes. This process will help you understand where you can cut back to increase your savings potential.

Saving will also change your mindset in terms of delayed gratification. As previously mentioned, instant gratification is very common and it can be addicting. If you want an item and have money in your wallet, why not buy it and get that rush of buying something new? Delayed gratification helps because you'll get more satisfaction from your purchases when you wait, research, and find the best deal. You'll feel proud knowing that you saved money and waited to ensure you really wanted or needed the item before buying it.

Automating Savings

Automating your savings streamlines the process. If your paycheck is directly deposited in your bank account, you can set up an automatic transfer that sends a portion of that money to your savings account online or through your bank app. This means you don't have to remember to log in and send a certain amount to your savings account. If you forget to do that, you might think the money in your account is everything you can spend so you'll fail to reach your savings goals.

If you already have a bank account, open another. If you're just getting started with banking, open a checking and savings account at once. Your checking account can be for the money you spend each month, and also where you'll deposit your paychecks. Then set up an automatic transfer to your savings account. Start with a standard amount you can easily afford. As you spend less and make more, increase your monthly savings deposits to increase your account over time.

Making Thoughtful Spending Choices

After shifting your mindset and automating savings, you'll find that it's easier to make thoughtful spending choices. You don't have to stop having fun and buying things you love, but you'll ensure everything aligns with your goals.

For example, you can create a budget that still allows you to spend money on fun activities and items you love as long as you also add a line item for savings. You can even put a certain amount in savings first and leave the rest of your income for whatever adventure you'd like to spend it on each month.

As long as you know the difference between your needs and wants, you'll feel empowered to make wise choices with your money. You should always prioritize your needs over your wants. Remember that you can eventually buy things you want from your savings, but thinking critically about what you want and why you want it will help you understand your purchases and can keep you from throwing your money away on items that you won't need next month or won't be in style next season.

When you spend money, shop smart. Look for deals and discounts before you buy. If you don't need to buy something right away, give yourself time to shop around or wait for it to go on sale. You can also shop secondhand or buy generic items instead of name brands to save money.

Saving goes beyond building a bank balance; you learn decision-making skills and money management approaches that you'll use for your entire life. Saving is the foundation of financial security, so starting while you're young gives you the tools you need to make your dreams a reality. It can seem challenging to save money, but after you change your mindset and automate the process, you'll find that you're on the right path to financial security and independence.

Activity

Automating savings is the best way to know you're constantly putting money into your savings account each month. It simplifies your budgeting work too because you're not having to move money manually. With that in mind, think of how much money you're able to save each month.

As mentioned in Chapter 3, the 50-30-20 budget is a very general approach that can help you understand the process as you refine it to suit your needs. The example used in that chapter had you making $1,000 a month and helped you understand how you could allocate that $300 for wants in any way you desired. There are many categories that fall within wants, so you could have some flexibility there.

A savings tracker separate from your budget can help you see exactly how much money you're putting away toward a goal or emergency fund. While you should still include savings as a line item on your budget, this worksheet can show you how much money you have, which can motivate you to continue saving even more. In this worksheet, you're going to list the things you need to save up for and use the 20% concept from the 50-30-20 guideline to divide your savings contributions into categories.

The blank in the three main columns refers to the savings type. Knowing exactly why you're saving can help give you a sense of purpose. Examples include:

- car down payment

- car insurance and gas

- college tuition

- concert tickets for your favorite band

- emergency fund

- new musical instrument/materials for your hobby

- road trip with friends

Fill in each category and go ahead and set your goal amount—but be realistic. If you're saving up for college, you won't save the full amount in one year, but you can aim to put away $3,000. Then write in the amount you deposit each month, after you save it. This differs from adding it to your budget up front because you only want to record it here after you actually save it. At the end of the year, add up all your deposits and see if you met—or exceeded—your goal!

	_____ Savings	_____ Savings	_____ Savings	Goal Amount	Actual Savings
January					
February					
March					
April					
May					
June					
July					
August					
September					
October					
November					
December					
Annual Total					

Chapter 6

SAY HELLO TO NEW FINANCIAL CONCEPTS

The information you've learned so far is fairly basic, taking ideas you already have about money and growing from there. But there may be some new financial concepts you're unfamiliar with, so this chapter will cover them. If you already know some of these terms, then read on for a refresher! These concepts give you a strong foundation of knowledge that will help you with budgeting, investing, saving, and more.

Banking Basics

Banking is simple, right? Open an account, deposit money when you have it, withdraw it when you need it. Sure, that's the basic idea, but you need to know what type of account to open. Savings accounts typically have a limit in terms of how many monthly transactions you can do, but they often have higher interest rates. Checking accounts include a linked debit card and allow more transactions, but they don't pay much in interest. If possible, you should get one of each account. Deposit money in your checking account for your bills and spending, and then transfer a set amount into your savings account each month where it will grow due to interest rates.

You should also learn everything about your chosen account. Some have set minimum balances, and if you go below that amount, you have to pay a fee. Some debit cards include fees if you withdraw cash from an ATM not linked with your bank. Otherwise, you can use a debit card to get cash or treat it like a credit card when paying for purchases.

You can monitor your bank account online through an official website or app. You'll need a personal identification number (PIN) and password to access your finances, and you shouldn't share that information with anyone. Check your account often to ensure all the purchases are ones you've made and no one has stolen your debit card number. Checking in will also help you stick to your budget.

All About Cards

Checking accounts are ideal because you can get a debit card, and purchases with cards are so much easier than using cash or checks. You can buy things online, fill up your gas tank at the pump without having to go into the store, and don't need to constantly withdraw and keep up with holding cash. Debit cards are better than credit cards because you can only spend the money in your account and there's less chance you'll overspend, but if you're financially responsible, you can have both cards at your disposal.

A debit card links to your bank account, allowing you to spend whatever money is in your account without needing to withdraw cash. However, you can withdraw cash from ATMs, typically for free if it's associated with your bank or for a small fee if it's not. You have a spending limit—the amount in your account—so this is a safe card to have as you learn to be responsible.

Credit cards have a spending limit, but it's much higher than what you have on hand. When you're 18, you can get credit cards with limits up to $4,000 or more, but that doesn't mean you should spend it! Remember that you have to pay back your credit card balance. If you can pay it off in full each month, you'll build a strong credit score. Always pay at least the minimum balance to stay in good standing with the company, but know that whatever you don't pay back will acquire interest, so you'll end up paying back more than your purchases actually cost.

When you're considering credit and debit cards, ensure you know the pros and cons of each.

Debit Card Pros:

- Debit cards are widely accepted by most online and in-person merchants.

- You won't accumulate debt because you spend what you have.

- You won't pay interest on your purchases.

- You can withdraw cash from ATMs with little to no fees.

Debit Card Cons:

- Debit cards won't help you build a credit score.

- You may encounter overdraft fees if you spend more than is in your account.

- They offer fewer rewards than credit cards.

Credit Card Pros:

- Credit cards are accepted almost everywhere online and in person.

- They build credit and boost your credit score with responsible use.

- They offer impressive rewards options like cashback and travel benefits.

- You have time to pay back what you spent.

Credit Card Cons:

- Purchases accumulate interest if you don't pay the balance by the due date.

- Available credit can tempt you to spend beyond your means.

- They often include fees if you try to use your card to get cash.

ATM Operations

ATMs are machines that allow you to pull out money from your checking account by using your debit card. You can find ATMs in most bank lobbies, grocery stores, gas stations, shopping centers, and many other stores and restaurants. If you want to use your bank's ATMs to avoid paying a fee, you can usually find a map of them on the bank's website.

At any ATM, you'll insert your card and then type your PIN. You'll get a PIN when you open your checking account and get a debit card, but you may have the ability to change the number online so it's something you easily remember. Never write your PIN on your card or let anyone see you input the numbers.

Once you sign in, the ATM gives you the option to withdraw cash, check your balance, transfer money, or deposit cash. When you finish the transaction, you can get a printed receipt or send it to the email you have on file with your bank. Keep this information for your expense tracking.

Taxes

You may not need to pay income taxes based on how much money you earn, but understanding the scope of taxes will set you up for financial success. There are also different types of taxes that you're most likely already paying.

For example, most stores and restaurants have sales tax, which is a percentage of your total bill. States and cities have their own sales tax rates. Some locations tax food and groceries at a lower rate than other goods to try and be accessible for all citizens. These taxes pay for local services like public safety, schools, road maintenance, and parks.

Income tax is what you pay every April. This money goes to the federal government to fund public services and infrastructure. Some states also have a state income tax, which you pay on top of the federal tax to fund your local needs. You'll need to file taxes annually, which you can do online for free through the IRS's website or by using a software program that walks you through the steps.

Your paycheck will also have Social Security and Medicare taxes taken out to fund your future. These deductions will provide money for your retirement and healthcare when you stop working. Once you become a property owner, you'll pay taxes based on the value of the home and land.

Loans

Loans are a great way to get access to money if you don't have the funds in your bank account. You can get loans for things like property, cars, and tuition. You can even get personal loans to help you reach financial goals, like taking a vacation or paying for your car repairs.

You can get a loan from a bank or other financial institution, but do your research to ensure they're a reputable company. You should also carefully consider the terms of the loan. The principal is how much you borrow, and you'll pay interest on that amount. If it takes you a long time to pay back a loan, you could pay much more than you borrowed. The term limit of the loan is stated before you accept the money, so you'll know how long you have to pay it back without major repercussions. However, you'll always pay interest on a loan, which you'll include in your monthly payments.

Since you'll pay interest on the loan, borrow only what you need. You might think it's cool that you can get a loan for $10,000 when you only need $3,000, but you'll pay interest on the total principal and that can be hard to pay back. Loans will show up on your credit report, but that's not necessarily bad. Paying back a loan can improve your credit score, so ensure you don't go into debt with a loan.

Insurance Policies

You may not think you need to know much about insurance as a teenager, especially if your parents cover your health insurance. However, knowing what to consider now can set you on the right path for the future. You'll eventually have to handle your own insurance, which includes health insurance, car insurance, and renters or homeowners insurance.

You need to have insurance to protect against major expenses.

For example, paying a monthly fee for health insurance protects you against a massive hospital bill if you get sick. Similarly, paying car insurance premiums means your insurance company will cover repairs if you get into a wreck. These are generalizations though, because each insurance policy has specific standards. You can choose a more affordable insurance plan to have coverage, but it might not pay for anything that happens to your health or car.

Before choosing an insurance plan, think of your needs. You might not need health insurance if you're a student and can stay on your parents' plan as a dependent, but you can check out their coverage to understand what you should look for when you find your own plan. Do the same research for car insurance. You can shop around to find the best deal for the most comprehensive coverage in any type of insurance. Once you commit to a plan, add the premium into your budget so you can always pay for insurance.

Digital Currencies

You can already bank online, so getting involved in digital currencies may interest you. This is also called cryptocurrency, which is a type of money that is purely digital. Instead of paying for something with dollar bills, you use electronic means protected with cryptography for online security. Bitcoin is the most well-known cryptocurrency, but there are plenty of other options, all with unique features.

Cryptocurrency uses blockchain technology that keeps track of all transactions in a decentralized way. Basically, this means that instead of tracking your spending through your bank account, each cryptocurrency contains all the transaction history it needs. Having digital funds can make it easier for you to grow wealth, but you need to understand the risks associated with this relatively new technology. The value fluctuates wildly, so you may pay a certain amount and watch the cryptocurrency lose its value quickly. However, if you're interested, researching the types of currency and buying from a reputable site can help you diversify your investments in trendy ways.

Smart Shopping

After learning how to budget in Chapter 3, you already have a new outlook in terms of the value of money and how you spend it. Even if you add room in your budget to spend money on new clothes, shoes, or entertainment, it's good to shop smart in the process. You can budget $100 and get a whole lot from the money, or get just one new item.

The key is planning what you want to buy and tracking expenses before you actually make the purchases. Give yourself time to research products to ensure you're getting the best quality, as these items will last longer and are worth the investment compared to cheap products that fall apart quickly. If you have time to wait, you may also find the item on sale or get a coupon you can use to save money.

When you shop for groceries, you should always make a list first. You can plan meals in advance to know what you'll eat all week and buy ingredients that help you reach this goal. It's so tempting to buy things that jump out at you at the store, especially junk food, but it's best to stick to the list to ensure you'll meet your budget.

These tips can help you negotiate better prices when you shop:

- **Research.** Gather information about typical price ranges for the product or service you're interested in. Knowing the market value is crucial. You can also check prices across stores to see if a different company offers lower prices. For example, some stores offer cheaper produce than others, or run specials on certain days.

- **Stick to your budget.** Think of how much you're willing to pay for something. If you really want organic produce, you need to know you'll pay more and budget accordingly, even if that means you skip getting meat or a treat from the store at the same time.

- **Shop seasonally.** You can typically find strawberries and peaches year-round at your grocery store, but if you buy them during winter, you're going to pay much more than you would in spring and summer. Consider buying the produce that's naturally available each season so you won't pay as much.

- **Buy in bulk.** If you're going to use a lot of food before it goes bad, you can save money buying in bulk. This includes rice, pasta, and canned goods. You'll spend less getting what you need, plus you'll have more for later.

- **Check unit prices.** While buying in bulk can often help you save money, for some products, you won't save more. You can check the unit price on the shelf label to see how much you're paying per item in a package. While larger packages often have a lower cost, that isn't always true, so it's best to check.

- **Use store benefits.** Many stores have membership programs like a card that comes with an app, digital coupons, and a point system. You can save points for discounts on your grocery bill or cheaper gas at the store's gas stations, helping you save more money overall.

- **Buy store brands.** Many people don't realize that store brands are just as good as name brands. In some cases, the same factory that produces the name-brand food also makes the store brand—the only difference is in the packaging (Black, 2023). That means you can save money buying store-brand food while still getting the same great taste of the name brand.

- **Buy whole fruits and vegetables.** It's convenient to buy pre-cut fruits and veggies to eat as snacks or use in recipes, but these options are more expensive. It's better to buy the full fruit or vegetable and cut it yourself. You'll have to put in some time and effort, but you'll save money.

- **Choose frozen or canned options.** While buying fresh produce is healthy and delicious, it can also get expensive. In many cases, you can choose frozen and canned options to save money and keep them longer. Many people buy fresh produce, but don't use it in time, so it wilts or goes bad, meaning they throw away their money as they throw away the food. Frozen and canned goods have a longer shelf life, so you don't have to worry about them going bad.

- **Ask for rain checks.** Sometimes a store will offer a coupon or discount that is so good, they quickly sell out of the item. In that case, you don't have to cut your losses and go home. Consider asking for a rain check, which means you'll get the sale price when the item comes back in stock, even if the promotion has officially ended by that point.

Scholarships

Paying for school is one of the biggest expenses you'll face as a teenager and new adult, but it's worth the investment if higher education is necessary for your personal goals and career path. You can attend a university, community college, or trade school and learn crucial skills that will help you secure the best jobs. However, these options are pretty expensive, so finding scholarships can help.

You can get financial aid based on your needs, earn scholarships because of your grades and accomplishments, or get money from community organizations. Research scholarships online, look at your ideal college for options, or talk to your counselor for resources. Always read the eligibility requirements to ensure you can get the scholarship, then prepare all the materials and meet the application deadline.

Start early when you're searching for scholarships and try any avenue you can find. The more money you get in scholarships, the less you'll have to pay up front for your education. Using scholarship money for school puts you in a great position for financial security in the future because you won't have student loans to pay back for years.

Look for scholarships offered by your chosen school, the community, private organizations, and the government. Online scholarship databases like Chegg, College Board, and Scholarship America can simplify the process. Check the eligibility requirements to ensure you can apply, then follow the instructions to fill out the document and attach other necessary information. Submit before the deadline and keep records of what you've applied for so you can track the scholarships you earn.

Credit Score

A credit score is like a grade for how well you manage your money. It's a three-digit number that shows how risky it is for a bank or lender to lend you money or give you a credit card. The higher your credit score, the better. It's like getting an A+ for handling your finances well, and it makes it easier to get loans and credit cards. But if your score is low, it's like getting a lower grade, and it can make it harder to borrow money. So, it's important to try to keep your credit score high by paying bills on time and being responsible with your money.

As a teenager, you won't have a credit score, but as you use a credit card and pay it off, you'll establish a score. When you behave responsibly and build a high credit score, you'll have more access to loans with lower interest rates because lenders won't see you as a risk. People with low credit scores have a harder time getting financial assistance and, once they do, they have a high interest rate that can put them in even more debt when they finally pay off the loan.

You can start building good credit now by asking your parents to add you as an authorized user on their credit card. You'll benefit from their credit history while having a safety net as you learn to use a credit card. You can also apply for your own student credit card with their approval. Pay all your bills on time, like your cell phone or credit card, which reflects positively on your credit score. Keeping all your outstanding balances low makes it easier to pay back and also boosts your score.

Interest Rates

Interest rates are like a fee you have to pay when you borrow money or the reward you earn when you save or invest money. When you borrow money, like getting a loan or using a credit card, you have to pay back the amount you borrowed plus an extra amount, which is the interest. It's like a cost for borrowing the money.

On the other hand, when you save your money in a bank account or invest it, the bank or investment might pay you interest. This is like a reward for keeping your money with them.

Interest rates sound boring, but they affect your money in many ways—some positively!

For example, a high-interest rate on your savings account means you'll make more passive income, or money without working for it, as you build your savings. However, a high-interest rate on your credit card means you're going to pay more on your outstanding balance. With that in mind, it's easy to see that you need to understand interest rates to make the most of your money.

Interest rates can be high or low, and they can change over time. If they're high, it can cost more to borrow money, but you might earn more when you save or invest. If they're low, borrowing money might be cheaper, but the rewards for saving or investing might not be as big. It's important to understand interest rates because they affect how much you pay or earn when it comes to money.

You might encounter interest on your credit cards, personal loans, and student loans. You'll have a positive experience with interest in terms of saving and investing because it helps you earn money. Regardless of when you encounter interest, you can make it work for you. Look for high-interest rates when you're investing, and low-interest rates when you're borrowing. Strive to pay off loans as soon as possible so you're only paying back what you borrowed, not the interest accumulated.

Inflation

Inflation is when the prices of goods and services go up and the value of money goes down. This means that with inflation, you might need more money to buy the same things you could have bought for less money in the past.

Imagine if a candy bar costs $1 today, but due to inflation, it costs $1.10 next year. You'll need more money to buy that same candy bar. Inflation can happen for various reasons, like an increase in production costs or too much money being printed, which can lead to the value of money decreasing.

For teens, it's essential to understand inflation because it affects your purchasing power, meaning how much you can buy with your money. If prices go up faster than your income, it can make it more challenging to afford the things you need and want.

Unfortunately, there's not much you can do to combat inflation. You may just have to tighten your budget or dip into savings to ensure you can still afford everything you need. You might have to change your future savings goals to keep a decent quality of life now. However, having a savings account or emergency fund can protect you in the case of inflation. Investing money in diverse outlets can also ensure you have enough money even if you don't get a raise at work.

Economic Cycles

An economic cycle, also known as a business cycle, is like the ups and downs of a roller coaster ride for our country's money. Sometimes the economy is booming, which means people have lots of jobs and businesses are making money. This is the "up" part of the cycle, and we call it an expansion.

But what goes up must come down, just like a roller coaster. So, the economy can also slow down, and when it really slows down a lot, we call it a recession. That's when it's harder to find jobs and businesses might not be doing as well.

After a recession, things start looking up again, which is the "up" part of the cycle, heading toward another expansion. This pattern of going up, then down, then up again is what we call an economic cycle. It keeps repeating over and over. Understanding these cycles helps grown-ups make decisions about the country's money to keep it on a smooth ride.

These cycles impact your earning potential and can influence your decisions in terms of when you decide to buy a car or house, what college to attend, and when to change careers. While you can't control economic cycles or truly prepare for them, you can constantly improve your education and upskill so you're ready to find a new job when necessary. Of course, financial securities like a savings account, emergency fund, and investments can also help you make it through a downturn.

Good and Bad Debt

Debt refers to money you owe someone else, whether it's a loan or a credit card balance. You may be in debt because of your student loans, your car payment, or your outstanding credit card debt. There's good debt and bad debt, so you want to spend carefully to ensure you're always financially secure.

When you have debt, you have less financial freedom than before. It will be harder to reach your goals, like buying a car or home. Your credit score can suffer when you have debt because you haven't paid back your loans, but as you pay it off, you'll improve your score. However, with a low credit score, it will be harder to get new loans, and they'll have high interest rates when you do. This can be a very stressful situation.

To avoid bad debt, borrow wisely and only as much as you need to reach your goal. Understand the terms of the loans and try to find the lowest interest rate. If at all possible, tighten your budget instead of taking out a loan. When you do borrow money, pay it back on time to eliminate debt and rebuild your credit score. This may mean you pay more than the minimum balance to show that you're willing to pay what you owe, and also reduces how much interest you'll pay.

Bad debt may include:

- extravagant car loans beyond the vehicle's value

- high amounts of outstanding credit card debt

- payday loans with high-interest rates

Good debt can include credit card balances that you repay each month or student loans because it shows you're boosting your future earnings potential and using borrowed money for good causes. Always carefully consider your needs before committing to a loan to ensure you're not taking on bad debt.

Good debt can include:

- business loans

- mortgages

- student loans

Net Worth

Your net worth is the difference between your assets and liabilities. Basically, your assets are valuable things you own, like your savings account and a car. Your liabilities are what you owe, like student loans and credit card debt. When you have more assets than liabilities, you have a higher net worth because you own more than you owe. This is a sign of financial health that bodes well for your future. You can strive to improve your net worth by budgeting and setting goals to increase your savings by a certain amount in the next year while also reducing liabilities.

People calculate net worth by adding all their assets, like savings accounts, investments, and property. Then they subtract everything they owe to someone else, whether it's a bank, credit card company, or friend.

For a teen, your net worth might not be very high because you're just starting to build your financial life. But it's a useful concept to understand as you grow older and start managing your money and assets. You can always change your net worth by saving, investing, reducing your debt, and spending less.

Opportunity Cost

Opportunity cost is what you give up when you decide to do something else.

For example, if you have an exam tomorrow, you can either decide to study tonight or go out with your friends. If you study, you improve your chances of getting an A on the test, but you miss out on a fun time with your friends. It's up to you to decide what matters most.

In financial terms, opportunity cost can greatly help you curb your spending habits. If you want to buy a new pair of shoes, you can see the value in fitting in with your friends or even being the envy of them if they don't have their own pairs. However, the shoes are so expensive that you'll have to work for 10 hours to pay for them. Another way to see the opportunity cost is to realize that buying these shoes means you won't be able to go with your friends to a concert next weekend because you don't have the money for the shoes and the ticket.

There's no real way to avoid opportunity cost because you're always going to have to make choices in life, choosing one option over another. However, you can use your financial literacy to weigh decisions and make the choice that will most positively impact your financial future. Always consider your short-term and long-term goals regarding opportunity cost.

Passive Income

Passive income is a way to make money without putting in much effort.

For example, you can build a website and host ads that earn money when other people visit your page. This is in contrast to your part-time job at the grocery store, where you earn money by stocking the shelves. The passive income continues to increase while you're doing other things—including sleeping!

If you can establish a way to make passive income, you'll greatly increase your earning potential. You can build wealth because you can make money at one job while your passive income accumulates in another field. It's another way to diversify your money, just like investing in stocks, bonds, and mutual funds.

As a teen, you might have limited ways to generate passive income. As previously mentioned, you can create a website or take stock photos and host them online. You can also host a blog, YouTube channel, or podcast that takes minimal effort but can generate ad revenue. As you increase your savings, you may want to invest in rental properties or loan money to other people or small businesses.

When it comes to making passive income, start small and make sure your approach is sustainable. You don't want to do something that requires more effort than you're able to put in. Research options and see what you can do for the long-term, as it often takes time to generate passive income—you're unlikely to get rich overnight!

Housing Costs

Housing costs refer to whatever you spend to have a place to live. They include the rent or mortgage you pay for a house or apartment, your utilities, any property tax, homeowners or renters insurance, and expenses relating to maintenance, repairs, and upkeep. Before you move out on your own, you need to consider all the expenses you'll encounter each month. There will also be some initial costs, like paying a security deposit and renting a moving van.

You'll need to consider these housing costs in your monthly budget. They'll be necessities, so factor them into your budget before anything else. You should strive to live somewhere you can afford, possibly getting roommates to help with the bills to ensure you can make ends meet and still save money to improve your financial future.

Before moving out, look around for different properties to get an idea of what you'll spend each month on rent. Some landlords will give you the estimated utilities if you ask, so you can factor that into your projected budget as well. Consider how much you make and how much you'll spend on these necessary expenses before signing a lease.

Activity

If you've opened your bank accounts and plan to regularly monitor your spending online, you need to develop a strong password. You don't want anyone to guess that your code is actually "password123" or your name and birth date. Passwords should be strong and unique so no one can guess them.

1. Look at these sample passwords and pick the one that would be the hardest to guess:

> 1. mypassword
>
> 2. 12345
>
> 3. 123abc
>
> 4. URdaB3st!

2. Answer these questions to create your strong password.

> 1. Favorite animal: _____
>
> 2. Favorite color: _____
>
> 3. Your age: _____

3. Now take your answers from question 2 and look for ways you can change the letters. For example, an "e" can be a "3" and a lowercase "i" could be an uppercase "I" or the number 1.

4. What letters can you replace in your password answers?

> • _____ for _____
>
> • _____ for _____

- _____ for _____

- _____ for _____

- _____ for _____

5. Finally, add a punctuation mark or special character. Try to choose one you love so you'll remember it, like an exclamation mark because you're always excited or a question mark because you're so curious. Put this at the beginning and/or end of your password to make it impossible to crack!

Since your password is a combination of things you love, you'll remember it easily, but no one else will be able to guess it. You can shuffle the information to start with your favorite color, animal, or punctuation—these questions are just a starting point!

Remember that this is just a practice exercise. You shouldn't write down your actual password anywhere because others can find and use it.

Chapter 7

Beware of Money
Minefields

Managing money can be tricky terrain, so watch out for minefields! There's a lot to learn as you strive for financial independence. Knowing what challenges to look for can help you stay on the right path, paying your bills each month while still saving toward your goals.

You're already learning financial literacy thanks to this book, so you have a solid foundation of knowledge to build on. From there, you'll learn about piling up payments, scams, impulse spending, and more. Don't let these land mines blow up your chance at financial security! Learn how to navigate your way around these obstacles safely.

Handling Debts

The best way to handle debt is to take on as little as possible. These tips will help you prevent and manage your debt.

- **Buy only what you can afford.** If you have a credit card, use it only to buy things you can pay back in a month to keep from having high-interest charges.

- **Find low interest rates.** If you need to borrow money, shop around for the lowest interest rates. This means you'll end up paying back less overall.

- **Only borrow exactly what you need.** This helps you pay it back as quickly as you can to prevent owing a lot of interest on the larger amount you borrowed.

- **Prioritize savings.** You can avoid most debts by prioritizing your savings or emergency account. If you have money to fall back on, you're less likely to need a loan if you have to pay for car repairs or an unexpected expense.

- **Budget your income.** Budgeting will help prevent debt because you can put money away for specific causes, like car insurance bills or medical checkup copays.

Poor Maintenance of Credit Scores

You may not think much of credit scores as a teenager because you haven't had time to build one. While the length of time can greatly improve your credit score, you can easily start off on a bad path with your first credit card. Some teens think a credit card is basically free money and don't consider how they not only need to pay for what they bought but will owe interest on those charges, too. That can add up quickly, especially if you only pay the minimum balance each month.

People develop bad credit scores for many reasons, including:

- maintaining a high credit card balance instead of paying it down each month.

- maxing out their credit cards, meaning they don't have enough cash to live so they charge everything, then struggle to pay it back.

- making late payments, which can also negatively impact your credit score. Aim to charge only what you can pay back.

- only paying the minimum balance each month. Paying over that amount is a simple way to boost your credit score.

You can maintain a good credit score with these tips:

- Pay bills on time, setting up automatic payments if you're worried you'll forget.

- Use less than 30% of your available credit and pay it back each month.

- Avoid opening too many credit accounts in a short amount of time.

- Keep older accounts open with manageable balances, as the age of your credit score matters.

- Review your credit reports from each agency annually to ensure they're accurate.

Lack of Planning and Budgeting

Budgeting can seem boring; you're young and want to have fun with your friends! That's understandable but planning ahead puts you on a more financially secure path to adulthood. You can budget your income now to start saving, giving your money more time to earn compound interest and create a passive income. Learning to budget is a skill that will serve you well later in life, too.

Teens who don't plan or budget may find themselves struggling to make ends meet. They may spend money for fun and then not have enough to fill their car with gas. They may constantly have to ask to borrow money, which can damage friendships if it's not paid back promptly. Teens who don't budget may simply miss out on a lot of fun because they're unable to go to movies or restaurants with friends, so they feel left out.

Overspending and debt are two of the biggest pitfalls when it comes to teen money management. Planning and budgeting can reduce both of these problems. When you create a budget, stick to it to ensure you're only spending what you can and are saving enough that you won't go into debt.

Piling Up Payments

The beauty of credit cards is that you can buy something now but pay for it later. However, if you allow payments to pile up, you won't have the necessary funds to pay things off. Having multiple debts at once will hurt your credit score and stress you out because you don't have a way to pay them back. You can work hard and put money toward repayment, but with interest rates, you'll soon be over your head and struggle to manage your money.

The best way to overcome the problem of piled-up payments is to only spend what you can afford. You can use a credit card to get the benefits but never spend beyond what's in your bank account or budget for a specific item. This practice guarantees you can always pay off the balance when the bill comes, so payments won't pile up.

The problem can be that you take on too much. Some teens have car payments, student loans, and credit card debt because they don't make enough to cover everything needed for their daily lives. You can consult a professional in the finance field to help you tackle these debts. It's possible to consolidate credit card debt onto one low-interest card and defer student loans until after graduation. Always ask for help if you're struggling instead of taking on more debt and trying to solve things yourself.

Poor Financial Knowledge

As previously mentioned, asking for help is the best solution when you don't know what to do. However, reading this book is already helping you combat the problem of having poor financial knowledge. You're learning about interest rates, debt, savings, and credit scores—topics many teens don't think about until they're on their own or already facing money struggles.

Money seems very straightforward—you earn it from working then spend it on things you need for your life or things you want. However, there are many intricacies relating to how credit cards and investments work. People who don't understand these concepts may end up overspending and accumulating debt, or investing more than they should and having money caught up in bonds without liquid funds to cover their cost of living.

The more you know about money, the more likely it is that you'll save money and achieve financial independence. Spend within your means and keep your debt low so you can start building wealth and have confidence in your budgeting and savings abilities, which can give you peace of mind instead of feeling stressed about your money.

No Savings

Saving money, even in small amounts, can set you up for financial success because the money adds up, can earn interest, and is in an account when you need it. Learning to save is just as important as how much you actually put away because it changes your mindset regarding money.

There are many reasons teenagers don't have savings. In some cases, they don't earn enough from their jobs to pay for their life. Some teenagers may impulsively buy items that they don't really need and some spend money as soon as they get it instead of putting it away for future needs.

Teens with no savings struggle with financial independence. They may not be able to afford everything they need. They might have to take out loans with high-interest rates to afford things and then struggle to pay back those loans. This lifestyle can cause a lot of stress, so it's better to start saving early and empower yourself to have a safety net when necessary.

As a teenager, you can set goals for your financial needs. Both long-term and short-term goals can require savings, so when you identify these expenses, you can budget around them to ensure your dreams come true. Automating savings will help you stay on track without requiring much upkeep and oversight.

Oversharing Personal Information

When it comes to financial matters, oversharing personal information doesn't mean you're telling your friends stories full of too much information (TMI). This type of TMI refers to data that someone can use to open accounts in your name or scam money from you. Think of the information you input when you open a new account, like your name, birth date, Social Security number, and more. Personal information can even include the passwords you use for mobile banking apps or PayPal, Venmo, and Cash App accounts. No one working at your bank will ever ask for your password over the phone or via text—that's a scam.

You shouldn't share your personal and financial information with anyone beyond the bank and credit card employees when you're setting up an account. When it comes to telling other people this type of information, you don't know how they'll use it. A friend may not believe you have the amount of savings you claim and wants your password to see proof, but even if you trust someone, you might prefer to sign into an app or account on your own device instead of giving them your password. However, there's no need to tell anyone about your financial status, so consider that personal information you should keep to yourself, too.

It's also possible to put too much information about yourself online in terms of your social media profiles or personal websites. You don't want to share so much that someone can piece together your first name, photo, and location and look you up online to get more data. Keep accounts private and only friend and message with people you know in real life to best protect your identity.

Risky Online Behavior

Sharing personal information online is risky behavior, but there are other things to be aware of, too. Online scams can allow people to steal your identity or hack into your accounts, so you need to be very cautious.

Scammers can be very crafty in how they get your personal information. Even in casual conversations, they may ask you questions about your first pet or your mother's maiden name, which are common password recovery questions on banking websites. They may pretend to have messaged you by accident and try to get access to your mobile banking apps to send themselves money. Always ensure you know who you're talking with online or in person and don't share personal information with others.

Hackers may email or text you links that look official but send you to a scam site, where they take your password, log into your account, and steal your funds. If you don't recognize an email address or phone number, it's best to ignore the message because of the risk of phishing attempts and malware installation on your devices.

You learned in Chapter 6 how to make a strong password that protects you from hackers. Consider changing your passwords every three to six months to add an extra layer of protection to your online accounts.

Falling Victim to Scams

Risky online behavior can make you fall victim to scams. Online scams trick people into giving away money or personal information so the scammer can benefit. There are many different types of scams, including the fake links and personal questions mentioned above. Some people may also hack into accounts by trying different passwords until they hit on yours, which is why the activity in Chapter 6 is so important for your security.

Some scammers go above and beyond, creating a fake online store. You can "buy" goods from the store and pay for them, but never get a delivery. The scammer takes your money and never sends any goods, often closing the store down shortly after to prevent you from contacting them for a refund.

Social media scams are also something to look out for, as they can be harder to detect. Some people will make fake accounts that look like your friend or family member. They may message you saying they were hacked or had their identity stolen and they don't have access to their original account anymore. They need money from you for a new phone or to hire a lawyer for help. You may trust them and send money before realizing it's a scammer posing as someone you know.

You should also be careful when using your credit card in person. When you hand it to a clerk, they may take a picture of the numbers or scribble them down to use later. Be especially cautious if they take your card out of sight and bring it back to you.

Not Seeking Financial Advice

Having the financial knowledge you're learning from this book may make you feel prepared for whatever comes your way, which is certainly the goal! However, there's no way to know everything, and you're still learning and experiencing things for yourself. There may come a time when you face an unfamiliar issue or are unsure how to handle a financial obstacle. At that point, you should seek financial advice. You can talk to your parents or guardians or make an appointment with a banker or financial advisor.

You may want to talk to a professional before you hit a roadblock. While this book provides quality information, some of it is general and your city or state may have different regulations involving minors opening banking or investment accounts. It's always better to ask for help and information before jumping in and getting in over your head, putting your finances at risk.

Impulse Spending

Impulse spending is one of the hardest things many people overcome on their way to financial security. It's easy to have a grocery list and get all the items you need, then feel tempted by a candy bar at the cashier's station and throw it in your basket just because. However, once you start doing this with small purchases, it's a slippery slope that may make you feel like it's okay to impulse buy larger items too. You get a rush when you buy something fun, and it can be addicting to experience this type of instant gratification. However, that gratification is very short-term and will wear off once the newness ends or you look at your budget and realize it's off for the month.

The best way to curb impulse spending is to make a budget and stick to it. When you go to a store, make a list of the things you need and only buy what's on the list. You may want to buy something to make yourself feel better if you have a bad day or see other people buying it. Advertising can also put a product in your head and make you think you need it because it improves your life. Never buy something in the moment; research it and think about it for a week to see if it's something you really need. Then ensure you can fit it into your budget without putting your financial security at risk.

Activity

Do you think you can avoid money minefields? Answer the following questions and see how you've built your financial knowledge.

1. You get a text from someone saying they're Laura, a teller at your bank. They know your name and the name of the bank. They ask for your password to ensure a recent, seemingly fraudulent charge of $1,000 didn't go through to your account. Do you text them your password?

   a. Yes

   b. No

2. A debit card pulls money from your bank accounts, while a credit card allows you to borrow money you may not have.

   a. True

   b. False

3. It's better to buy what you need as soon as you need it instead of saving money for potential emergencies.

   a. True

   b. False

4. If you don't have the money for something you want to buy, what should you do?

   a. Ask a friend to borrow money.

   b. Take out a loan.

   c. Assess why you need the item and try to go without it.

5. You maxed out one credit card and have three bills you need to pay before next week. What do you do?

   a. Pay the minimum balance on the credit card.

   b. Let the bills wait and pay for your immediate necessities.

   c. Contact a financial advisor for help managing your debt.

Answers:

1. b, 2. a, 3. b, 4. c, 5. c

Chapter 8

TIPS TO ATTAIN FINANCIAL FREEDOM

At your age, the idea of financial freedom may seem unattainable or something to worry about later. You have a lot in your future that requires saving, spending, and loans, so you might think that financial freedom is unattainable until you become wealthy. However, starting now with budgeting and saving makes it more likely you'll attain financial freedom sooner rather than later.

The goal of financial freedom is to make choices based on your goals instead of feeling restricted by money or financial obligations. These practical tips will help set you up for security and independence as you transition into adulthood.

Earn Your Money Efficiently

Earning money efficiently now increases your potential to build wealth in the future. You'll have the means to achieve your goals while also understanding valuable life skills about what you're worth and how you can make the most of your potential. Start with part-time jobs, volunteer positions, and any opportunity that utilizes your skills and gives you experience. You can leverage this to get better-paying jobs, start side hustles, and even form your own business.

Doing this efficiently means you're not spending 10 hours a day working hard for minimum wage. It means you're saving or investing money to earn interest. It includes seeking financial aid and scholarships for college tuition. It means you're working smarter, not harder, finding ways to earn passive income and build wealth while also sticking to a budget to ensure you live within your means.

Manage Your Finances Well

Earning money is just part of the journey to grow wealth; you need to manage your finances well so you don't spend more than you have. Budgeting is key to this, which is why it's the first skill you learned in this book. You need to assess how much money you earn and spend so you can tighten up where it's necessary and start saving to acquire wealth. After budgeting, saving is the best way to manage your finances. Even if you keep money in a savings account, it will stay protected and earn interest while you spend within your means.

Setting goals will greatly help you manage finances because you'll have something to look forward to. You may want to buy a new car, pay for your degree without student loans, or buy a house or rental property. Having both long-term and short-term goals can inspire you to be more frugal because you know being strict now will pay off in the future.

When it comes to managing your finances, you don't have to be a spreadsheet master. Financial apps are incredibly helpful when it comes to budgeting, automating savings, and tracking your spending. Work smarter, not harder, by utilizing these services to manage your money.

Some apps to check out include:

- EveryDollar

- Expensify

- Greenlight

- Mint

- Rocket Money

Donate Your Money for a Good Cause

After so much information on savings, investments, and compound interest, it might seem backwards to encourage you to donate your money! However, making a positive impact on the world will make more of a difference than keeping all your money in your bank account. When you save money, you serve yourself. When you donate to a good cause, you serve others and can make a major difference in someone's life.

Look for organizations that align with your values. Are you passionate about animals or education? There may be local organizations that serve these populations, so you can see your money make a difference in your community. You can also donate to national or global companies online to make a difference far from home. When you make online donations, follow the best practices as outlined in the previous chapter for protecting your password and personal information. You can also do research on your chosen nonprofit to ensure the bulk of their funding goes to their cause, not the people working in administration.

Avoid Wasting Money

Defining a "waste of money" will vary according to person, so you'll need to think about what makes you feel like you're throwing money away. Is it when you splurge on a new pair of shoes, only to see that they go out of style the next month? Is it when you buy a shirt and see that it's falling apart after the first wash? Knowing what is a waste of your money will help you make smart decisions when you're buying goods and services.

Impulse purchases are frequently a waste of money because you're buying something on the spur of the moment instead of researching it. The company may not produce high-quality products, or it might not be something you use much. Keeping a budget and tracking your spending prevents wasting money because you always prioritize your needs over your wants. You know how much money you want to save and why, and that idea of security and reaching a goal makes it easier to say no to wasting money.

Tackle Debts Properly

Having debt isn't the end of the world, especially since paying off debt can boost your credit score and make you more appealing to lenders! You need to understand how to manage them to ensure they benefit you.

For example, you may think you need to start chipping away at your biggest debt first, but in reality, you should consider the interest rates. The debt with the highest interest rate is what you should pay off quickly because that means you'll pay less overall.

When you have debt, you should revise your budget and factor in paying off this money just as you would add categories for bills and savings. It might mean tightening your expenses for a few months, prioritizing paying off debt instead of going out with friends. You may even shave some money off your savings deposits to ensure you won't spend too much on interest fees. While you're tackling debt, ensure you spend well within your budget so you don't accumulate even more debt!

Explore Entrepreneurship

You may feel limited in terms of money-making opportunities, so consider exploring entrepreneurship. This gives you the chance to focus on your skills and talents and create a business. You can do this in your free time while holding down more traditional employment, maximizing your earning potential. Or you may find that being your own boss gives you the chance to make more money than you could as someone else's employee!

Consider your skills and how you can use them to make money, sell goods, or offer a service. Maybe you love to clean or mow yards. You might have talents as a photographer or graphic designer. Start with your talents and things you love to do and think creatively about how people may pay for these services.

The biggest benefit of entrepreneurship is that you do more than earn money. You learn how to run a business, solve problems, and think innovatively. These skills all lead to personal growth that will serve you well in the future. You don't have to run your own business forever, but it can be a great chance to learn and explore while you're a teenager.

Stay Focused on Long-Term Goals

As a teenager, your life is busy with school, work, friends, family, and planning for the future. Long-term financial goals may be at the bottom of your to-do list, if you consider them at all. However, they're actually some of the most important things you should think about as you transition into independent living.

Knowing that you have set goals to accomplish in the coming years can motivate you, whether they relate to college, your career path, or moving out of your parents' home. You'll have something to work for, and every dollar you save gets you a step closer to making that dream a reality.

Set clear goals so you know what you're working toward and visualize that success. When you can picture what a difference that goal will make in your life, you'll have a sense of purpose that keeps you on the right path.

Learn From Mistakes

When you're dealing with money, you may think that everything has to go smoothly or else you'll end up in financial ruin. However, the beauty of earning, spending, and investing money is that you'll always have a chance to learn from your mistakes. While information like this book will help you gain basic knowledge, you'll learn even more when you're managing your money hands-on.

For example, you can read about investments in Chapter 4, but you don't really know what it's like until you buy shares in stocks or allow a financial advisor to invest money on your behalf. Then you get a chance to see the reality of how your money can grow and decrease with the market, and you'll be able to track short-term and long-term fluctuations. If you buy a stock that doesn't perform well, you learn from the experience and can pull your money out and invest in something else.

Resilience is key when it comes to financial success. You should never feel content with where you are money-wise because you can always do more. Budget more for savings, ramp up your investments or donate more to a cause that means a lot to you. Whenever you make a mistake, learn from the error, dust yourself off, and keep moving forward to stay on the right financial path.

Invest Wisely

As previously mentioned, investments can feel like a positive way to make money or a way to stress yourself out when you watch the market rise and fall. If you do research ahead of time or find a trusted financial advisor, you can invest wisely and know your choices will pay off in the long run.

Try the activity at the end of Chapter 4 for several months in a row, tracking different stocks each time. This will help you notice patterns and better understand how your investments can grow. Start small when you invest your money so you won't lose much if you make a mistake. When you feel like you're unable to make the right choices, ask for help so you can learn from a professional and get the most out of your investments.

Invest in Education

One thing that is always a smart choice is investing in education. When you learn, you greatly increase your earning potential because you have new skills and talents that help you make money. You're empowered to learn and appreciate personal growth, which will help you feel more confident in terms of your personality as well as your finances.

You can invest in education by setting goals related to your budget and career goals. Maybe you want to attend a four-year university program and later earn higher degrees. You might want to take advantage of your state's free tuition for community college and get a terminal degree that prepares you for a job. You might want to save money to take courses and earn certificates well into adulthood so you always stay on the cutting edge of your field.

Be Patient

As a teenager, you may want to have everything now, and waiting seems impossible to handle. You need to remember that wealth isn't immediate; it takes time and effort to grow. However, while you're being patient, you can also be proactive in terms of earning money and establishing financial security.

The tips in this chapter greatly help you understand the small steps you can take that will pay off over time. You can empower yourself to have money now, which alleviates stress, while saving for the future to have a safety net for adulthood. By saving, budgeting, avoiding impulse purchases, investing, and educating yourself, you'll take the right steps toward financial independence and wealth in time.

Activity

Your goal is to achieve and maintain financial freedom, but that's easier said than done. You might want to build wealth, but you still want to live a good life and enjoy every day. With that in mind, listing your needs and wants and balancing them to ensure you have everything you need, but also some things you want, can help you love your life while still setting yourself up for financial success. This activity will help you assess your needs and wants and allow you to fit them into your budget.

1. What is your monthly income (part-time job, allowance, etc.)?

2. How much do you pay for necessary expenses, like cell phone bills, public transportation, gas, car payments, etc.?

3. How much do you put into savings each month?

4. How much do you have left to spend however you choose?

5. Write a list of things you would buy if you had the money and how much each item would be. Be realistic.

Highlight things on your list that are closer to your needs, whether they refer to food or entertainment that makes you enjoy your life the most. Mark through the items that are wants, or things you can easily live without and still have a great life.

Look at the highlighted items and see what you could fit into your budget. Things that aren't too expensive may be something you can buy now or with your next paycheck. Items that cost a bit more could go into your budget as a temporary item so you can save money until you buy them.

Take this approach when there's something you want to buy but you don't have the funds right away or aren't sure if you should splurge on it. Because you're taking time to think critically about the items, they're more likely to be things you'll truly love. You may also take that time to shop around and find a discount code or wait until they're on sale, which can help your financial stability even more!

Chapter 9

BENEFITS OF LEARNING
MONEY SKILLS

Learning money skills at a young age gives you the knowledge you need to build a successful financial future and empowers you to make smart decisions about your money. The previous eight chapters of this book have given you financial knowledge that goes hand in hand with other life skills you've learned by now and will continue to learn well into adulthood. Since you're starting your years of teenage life and the transition to independence with this information, you can see how much hard work you should put into money management—and also see how much it will pay off!

Provides Financial Literacy

Financial literacy means you understand the concepts and tools relating to money management. You know how to create and stick to a budget and understand why this skill will help your finances. Information about saving and investing gives you perspectives regarding how you can make your money work for you, thanks to learning about compound interest.

The earlier you start tracking your expenses and prioritizing saving, the more prepared you are for the future. Before you know it, you'll be paying for college, buying a home, supporting a family, and retiring in comfort. Financial literacy is the key skill that helps you reach those goals.

Makes Teens Independent and Empowers Them

Money skills empower you because it fosters independence and responsibility. The more you understand how to manage your money, the better prepared you are for the things that come your way.

For example, learning how to budget helps you stretch your income and ensures you can buy what you need, which serves you well when you live independently and need to pay rent, utilities, and other bills.

As you create a budget, you understand the importance of setting goals to reach in the future. When you earn money, you respect the value of it in a different way. Everything you learn about money empowers you to change your mindset and make wise decisions.

Builds Your Identity

Money skills help build your identity because you'll understand yourself in a different way. You have goals and values that you stick to in order to create a specific life for yourself. When you can responsibly handle your money, you empower yourself to be confident and capable, which then reinforces your positive financial choices.

You can respect hard work and the value of earning money while also enjoying a passive income thanks to smart investments. Every way you interact with money in your life impacts your financial values and sets you up for future success as the person you want to become.

Instills Accountability

When you earn and spend your own money, you appreciate the accountability. Instead of asking your parents to buy something for you or having to borrow money from friends, you're accountable for your own purchases in a way that empowers you to make smart decisions.

Handling your own money also helps you understand consequences. It only takes once to spend more than you have and owe someone to realize that you should have a better handle on your finances. Once you start budgeting, saving, and setting goals, you change your mindset in a way that keeps you accountable across the board.

Helps Overcome Monetary Fraud

Your financial awareness can protect you against fraud and scams. You learned about some common approaches in Chapter 7, but scammers will always find new ways to try and steal money. Just knowing what they're capable of can help you stay aware of what's going on in relation to your personal information and finances.

When you regularly track your spending and stick to a budget, you'll notice when there's a strange purchase on your credit card statement or a large withdrawal from your bank account. You can find the root of any problem quickly because you're actively engaged with your money. Financial literacy can protect you from fraud and scams by promoting critical thinking and ensuring you're aware of what's happening in the financial landscape.

Teaches Ways to Handle Financial Emergency

No one plans for an emergency, which is exactly why having an emergency fund is so important. You can create a strict budget every month, but you'll eventually have unexpected medical bills or car repairs that require more money than you typically have in your budget. This is where an emergency fund is crucial. When you've been budgeting money for savings each month, you're going to have a nest egg ready to help you pay for those emergency expenses.

You can handle financial emergencies even without a safety net by tightening your budget and cutting out unnecessary expenses until you handle unexpected costs. Your financial literacy and practice, with all the skills you've learned in this book, empower you to take a flexible, creative approach to your money, ensuring you can handle whatever comes your way.

Assists in Making Accurate Financial Decisions

Your financial knowledge helps you make accurate decisions. You always understand how much money you're earning, how much you have in your accounts, and what you've invested. This full picture of your funds helps you make the best choices for goals in your life.

For example, if you've invested $1,000 in a CD to earn a high-interest rate for two years, you'll know you'll have several thousand dollars to put toward your college education. You'll also know that you need to rely on your other accounts to pay for necessities until you can withdraw the money from the CD because it's tied up in that fund.

Having a broad view of your current finances helps you plan ahead because you can set goals, assess the risks you're willing to take, and budget to ensure you stay in good financial standing. This approach also helps you develop strategies to grow your wealth by investing small amounts and keeping other amounts accessible for your needs.

Helps in Long-Term Wealth Building

Even if you win the lottery, you won't really become wealthy in one fell swoop. You might get a chunk of money at once, but it takes financial literacy to manage the money and ensure it doesn't run out quickly. With that in mind, you can appreciate how building wealth is a long-term goal that you can only achieve with the strong financial foundation you've been creating in this book.

You can't save money without income, and Chapter 2 helped you understand the kind of work you can do. Once you make money, you need to understand budgeting, saving, and investing so you can be smart with your income. Understanding the risks involved with online interactions and investing without research also empowers you to build wealth because you know what scams to be aware of and what things you shouldn't do for the best financial health.

Helps Develop Responsible Consumer Behavior

Companies are in it to make money, so it's up to you to develop responsible consumer behavior and control your spending. Brands design ads to convince you that their product is the best thing ever and that it will change your life, but you have the power of critical thinking on your side. The whole shift in your financial mindset that this book inspired will help you research the brand and product before you throw away your money. You can look to see what it actually does and assess if you need it in your life. You can read reviews and try to find more affordable options, or search for a coupon to help you save money.

When you think critically about purchases before you make them, you're being a responsible consumer. You're assessing your needs versus your wants and staying aware of how much money you have in your budget for that type of purchase. Even if you decide to buy the item, you can feel confident because you thought about it before making an impulse purchase.

Reduces Stress

Even though money may not buy happiness, it can certainly cause stress. When you hone your financial literacy and practice smart budgeting, you reduce your stress and anxiety revolving around money. You'll always know how much money you make each month and where it goes. Budgeting means you cover your bills first, so you have a sense of security in terms of your cell phone bills, car payments, savings accounts, and other necessary expenses.

When you save and invest money to grow wealth, you reduce your stress even more because you're preparing for the future. You're making long-term goals and planning how you can make them a reality. Instead of living paycheck to paycheck, you're establishing an emergency fund that will protect you in a financial crisis.

Supports Goal Achievement

Money skills help you achieve your goals because you understand how you need to take steps toward reaching your dreams. You can have a plan in mind and take action bit by bit, saving money to pay off debt or make a major purchase. You can prioritize your goals based on their importance or timelines and change your approach to saving money.

It's easy to think that money can solve problems and help you reach goals, but that's not the point here. It's more about how you handle yourself and your finances to plan ahead and ensure you're empowered to make good choices in life. Being financially independent is a major goal to reach because you want to be responsible for your own life instead of depending on others to loan you money or help you out in various ways.

You'll learn how to track your progress in terms of monitoring your expenses and watching your savings account grow. These skills help you appreciate delayed gratification, which you'll feel as you work toward a major goal and then find yourself accomplishing something you've wanted for months or years. You'll understand how meaningful this feeling truly is compared to the fleeting sensation of instant gratification.

Activity

Before you buy anything, you need to demonstrate responsible consumer behavior, use your financial literacy, and make wise choices for each purchase. This activity will help you follow the steps that set you on the right path to buy something that suits your needs and will last a long time without draining your bank account. Whether you want to buy something majorly expensive or simply buy a cute trinket, take time to think it through before handing over your hard-earned money.

For each potential future purchase, ask yourself the following questions:

1. What do I want to buy?

2. Why do I need it?

3. What is my budget?

4. What are my criteria for this purchase?

5. What are my top three choices, and how much is each?

6. Decide on my final choice!

Keep these questions on hand so you can work through each purchase before you make it.

Chapter 10

A BIG NO TO
MONEY-RELATED MYTHS

Even with the financial literacy you've learned while reading this book, it's still easy to fall prey to myths and misconceptions about money. You might think you need to earn a big salary to save money, or that you should avoid all debt at any cost (no pun intended). These myths can have a big impact on your financial decisions, so it's important to debunk them and ensure you have a more informed approach to your money matters.

Making a Budget Is a Strenuous and Lengthy Task

Budgeting was tackled early on in this book because it's such a crucial step in money management. Many people think making a budget is hard work and takes forever, but you'll find that's not true when you sit down and get to work. It might take a bit of time to create your initial budget because it's something new to you, but it gets easier. In fact, budgeting can save you time because you don't have to scrounge around for money or try to remember where you spent your last $20—you've tracked it all in your budget! You're less likely to make late bill payments or stress over expenses because you already planned for things in the budget.

In time, budgeting becomes even easier. For the first few months, you'll want to check in regularly to ensure you're spending within your means. Eventually, you may find that you don't need to set aside money for restaurants because you prefer eating at home. Or you may tighten your budget if you're saving for a big-ticket item. You can also save time by using a budgeting app that links to your bank account and credit cards to track your expenses for you. It won't take much time at all to oversee your budget once you get into the right money-saving mindset!

Money Can Buy Everything

It's true that money can buy a lot and alleviate plenty of stress, but it can't buy everything. Money can repair your car if you're in a wreck, but it can't buy your health and happiness. Other factors influence that aspect of your life, like eating a balanced diet, exercising, getting plenty of sleep, and spending time with loved ones. While you focus on your financial wellness with this book, ensure you're also making time for self-care, giving yourself space to relax, read a book, listen to music, play a game, and unwind.

Money can't buy things like time or love. While making money is a great way to establish financial security, working all the time shouldn't be your priority. You have a limit of 24 hours a day, so you should balance them carefully to ensure you do the things you need to do, but also have time to be with your loved ones and enjoy your hobbies.

If you've ever made impulse purchases, you understand how money can only provide a temporary thrill without long-lasting emotional fulfillment. It's too easy to think that a certain product will change your life and make you happy or more efficient, but it rarely delivers. Your true happiness won't come from money but rather from pursuing goals that matter to you and finding your purpose in life.

All Cards Are Alike

Besides the color and logo, most cards look alike, but they're very different. First of all, there are credit and debit cards. They're both plastic and the same size, but if you try to make a major purchase, one might go through and the other probably won't! That's because credit cards are like temporary loans, while debit cards pull money from your checking account. Credit cards offer different rewards programs. Some let you earn cash back for each dollar you spend, while others offer rewards for specific things, like travel or retail purchases.

Scammers can steal your information from both credit and debit cards, so you should closely monitor your accounts to watch for fraud. Many banks and credit card companies offer monitoring services, so look for this perk to ensure you're not held liable for charges a criminal makes on your card.

All Debt Is Bad

Debt might seem like a bad idea because it means you owe someone money, but in reality, you're going to owe money at some point in your life. It's tough to buy a house in cash, so you'll most likely need to take out a loan for this type of major purchase. Fortunately, there are good debts like mortgages, student loans, and business loans. You're borrowing money to improve your status in life, so you're increasing your earning potential and building equity with these loans.

Bad debt only refers to things that aren't valuable and may put you in financial trouble.

For example, maxing out a credit card buying the latest tech isn't a good choice and will become nearly impossible to pay off due to the interest rates. Getting a loan for a luxury car that loses over half its value as soon as you drive it off the lot is another instance of bad debt because you could have bought a more affordable car that retained value and not needed as high of a loan.

Make wise decisions when you realize you need a loan to ensure you're taking on good debt instead of bad. You should shop around and find the best interest rate. If you make regular payments on your loan, it's a perfectly acceptable way of making a big purchase and reaching your financial goals.

A Higher Salary Means You'll Save More

Making more money always sounds like the best choice, right? While you should get paid what you're worth, which means you need to make a living wage, earning a higher salary doesn't automatically mean you can save more money. First off, making more money means you'll pay more taxes because you're in a higher income bracket.

Secondly, if you start your career making a lot of money, it might be hard to change your habits and live a more financially conscious lifestyle.

For example, if you get a huge first paycheck and spend it on nice work clothes and then lease a fancy car with your next paycheck, you're more likely to want to spend your future income right away. With so much money coming in each month, it can be tough to tell yourself you need to save a portion of it because you feel financially secure based on your monthly income.

Basically, even if you make a high salary, there are still going to be unexpected expenses in your life. You may encounter an emergency that requires thousands of dollars for a car repair or medical expense. While your salary may give you more resources to work with, it's still up to you to curb your spending habits and prioritize saving, so a higher income doesn't necessarily mean you'll save more.

Activity

A higher salary doesn't necessarily mean you'll save more because you might have a more expensive lifestyle. However, choosing a career that pays well can have a positive impact on your financial freedom. While doing something you love for work will make you feel like you enjoy life more than if you hate your job, you should also consider how much you can make in each field.

This worksheet will help you assess possible career paths for your future and give you an idea of what financial security you may have with each job. Fill in the job title and research the role on the U.S. Bureau of Labor Statistics and the Career Profiles websites. If you know anyone working in these industries, see if they'll meet with you to give information about what they earn and the work they do.

Job Title	Hourly Wage (if applicable)	Low-End Salary	Median Salary	High-End Salary

While this table doesn't tell you what career to pursue, it can help you make a decision. You should do something you love and are good at, but if you'll financially struggle in life, that might be a better choice as a hobby or side job, and you can focus on a higher-paying job as your main source of income.

CONCLUSION

This book has taken you on an impressive journey relating to money, from helping you find work to starting to earn your own income to investing wisely so your money works for you! You've learned the intricacies of interest rates, investment options, and budgeting. You've developed a new understanding of the value of money and how you can get the most from every dollar you make. The information in this book shows you that budgeting isn't just about crunching numbers, but more about making informed decisions and thinking critically about what you want and why. Taking time to research potential purchases and investments will help you create a more secure future.

Teenagers often feel like the world of finance is something they can't dive into yet because they don't have much money, but this book shows you how important it is for you to take control of your finances now! You can start earning money in different ways, even if you're not old enough for standard employment—start your own business or create a side hustle based on your skills and talents! Save or invest money now so it can start earning compound interest that can end up adding thousands of dollars to your retirement account decades down the line. The habits you develop now will shape your financial future, so you should follow the advice in this book and make consistent, smart choices regarding your money.

Above all, remember that financial freedom isn't only about how much money you have, but rather the choices you make with those funds. You want the freedom to reach your goals and make decisions that align with your values so you get the most of your money, whether that means you pay for college, start a business, or travel the world. Financial stability is the foundation that can help you achieve anything you put your mind to.

Though you've reached the end of this book, you still have the power to continue learning more about finance with your hands-on experience. Set goals that will help you live a great life with a financial security net beneath you. The path to mastering money is ongoing, and you'll encounter obstacles along the way. However, you can always learn from your mistakes and keep moving forward, making different choices and exploring your options. Financial freedom means you have control over your money, so you should use your knowledge, determination, and mindset to impact your future. Though you may struggle along the way, your wisdom empowers you to make changes to your lifestyle, make cents of your dollars, and create the life you want to live. Your financial journey starts here, and your possibilities are limitless!

Thank you for reading this book. I know finances may seem like a tough subject, but learning all you can now will make a huge difference in your future. If this book helped you, please leave a review sharing your experience! I love hearing from readers, and reviews will help other teens find this book and boost their financial literacy just as you have!

I'D LOVE TO KNOW WHAT YOU THINK!

Thank you for reading my book. I hope you enjoyed it!

Writing this book was a labor of love, and I poured my heart into every chapter. As an independent author, your feedback means the world to me. I would be immensely grateful if you could please take a few moments to share your thoughts in a review.

Reviews are crucial in supporting authors like myself and helping other teens discover this book. I genuinely read every review and am excited to hear your thoughts.

Thank you!

Ready to share your thoughts? Scan one of the QR codes below:

Amazon US

Amazon UK

Amazon Canada

Amazon Australia

REFERENCES

Adams, R. (2023a, September 27). *40 ways to make money as a teenager [fast + smart, 2023]*. Young and the Invested. https://youngandtheinvested.com/ways-to-make-money-as-a-teenager/

Adams, R. (2023b, September 27). *Best investments for teenagers [what to invest in as a teen]*. Young and the Invested. https://youngandtheinvested.com/best-investments-for-teenagers/

Allinson, M. (2023, January 18). *Why is money important in our lives?* Robotics & Automation News. https://roboticsandautomationnews.com/2023/01/18/why-is-money-important-in-our-lives/59144/

Attkisson, A. (2023, July 16). *Teaching kids about money: An age-by-age guide*. Parents. https://www.parents.com/parenting/money/family-finances/teaching-kids-about-money-an-age-by-age-guide/

Avallone, M. (2016, June 7). *5 financial concepts to teach your teen before high school graduation.* Forbes. https://www.forbes.com/sites/markavallone/2016/06/07/five-financial-concepts-your-teens-should-understand-before-high-school-graduation/

Beattie, A. (2023, April 5). *5 simple ways to invest in real estate*. Investopedia. https://www.investopedia.com/investing/simple-ways-invest-real-estate/

Behringer, E. (2020, May 18). *Top financial concepts every teen should know*. Linkedin. https://www.linkedin.com/pulse/top-financial-concepts-every-teen-should-know-eddie-behringer/

Black, M. L. (2023, May 10). *Store brand vs. name brand: What to know before you shop*. Taste of Home. https://www.tasteofhome.com/article/s

tore-brand-vs-name-brand-foods/

Blum, D. (2020, February 18). 5 big myths about money and parenting. *The New York Times*. https://www.nytimes.com/2020/02/18/parenting/money-savings-children.html

Brin, C. (2023, May 22). *Ultimate guide to budgeting for young adults & teens*. Hyperjar.com. https://hyperjar.com/blog/money-management-ultimate-guide-to-budgeting-for-young-adults-and-teens

Brock, R. (2023, May 31). *Understanding risk vs reward*. The Motley Fool Australia. https://www.fool.com.au/investing-education/understanding-risk-vs-reward/

Bromberg, M. (2023, March 10). Investing for teens: What they should know. *Investopedia*. https://www.investopedia.com/investing-for-teens-7111843

Chanda, P. K. (2023, February 17). Importance of money. *The Times of India*. https://timesofindia.indiatimes.com/readersblog/blogs-of-preetish/importance-of-money-50590/

Choudhury, K. (2021, March 24). *What are the benefits of budgeting?* Cabot Financial. https://www.cabotfinancial.co.uk/money-management/money-management/what-are-the-benefits-of-budgeting

Cruze, R. (2023, September 29). *15 practical budgeting tips*. Ramsey Solutions. https://www.ramseysolutions.com/budgeting/the-truth-about-budgeting

Danielsson, M. (2022, September 23). *How to reach financial freedom: 12 habits to get you there*. Investopedia. https://www.investopedia.com/articles/personal-finance/112015/these-10-habits-will-help-you-reach-financial-freedom.asp

DeMatteo, M. (2020, December 24). *At what age should you start teaching your child about credit?* CNBC. https://www.cnbc.com/select/teaching-children-about-credit/

Dhapai, H. (2023, April 25). *Top 13 skills to make money every student must know*. IIDE. https://iide.co/blog/top-5-skills-for-students-to-make-real-money/

Dhoke, M. (2023, May 13). *5 money management myths that can upset your financial well-being*. Personal FN. https://www.personalfn.com/dwl/Financial-Planning/5-money-m anagement-myths-that-can-upset-your-financial-well-being

Egan, J. (2021, November 22). *ATMs (automated teller machines): What are they?* Forbes Advisor. https://www.forbes.com/advisor/banking/atm -automated-teller-machine/

Ezeagwuna, C. (2023, August 22). *How to earn money as a teenager*. Kids' Money. https://www.kidsmoney.org/teens/earning/

Fagan, D. (2020, January 29). *Real-life examples of opportunity cost*. St. Louis Fed. https://www.stlouisfed.org/open-vault/2020/january/real-lif e-examples-opportunity-cost

Fernando, J. (2023a, March 30). *Financial literacy: What it is, and why it is so important*. Investopedia. https://www.investopedia.com/terms/f/fi nancial-literacy.asp

Fernando, J. (2023b, August 11). *Inflation: What it is, how it can be controlled, and extreme examples*. Investopedia. https://www.investoped ia.com/terms/i/inflation.asp

Fowler, J. (2022, November 27). *10 common scams targeted at teens*. Investopedia. https://www.investopedia.com/financial-edge/1012/com mon-scams-targeted-at-teens.aspx

Frazier, L. (2023, February 1). *Why teenagers should start investing early...and 3 proven investment tips for any age*. Forbes. https://www.forbes.com/sites/lizfrazierpeck/2023/02/01/why-teenagers -should-start-investing-earlyand-3-proven-investment-tips-for-any-age/?s h=2b79711b70e0

Gobler, E. (2022, June 20). *Investing guide for teens (and parents)*. The Balance. https://www.thebalancemoney.com/investing-guide-for-teens-and -parents-4588018

Gregoire, C. (2018, February 8). *How money changes the way you think and feel*. Greater Good. https://greatergood.berkeley.edu/article/item/how_ money_changes_the_way_you_think_and_feel

Grossman, A. L. (2022, November 29). *9 reasons to save money as a teenag-*

er (use these talking points). Money Prodigy. https://www.moneyprodigy .com/reasons-to-save-money-as-a-teenager/

Grossman, A. L. (2023, January 6). *How to teach your teenager the value of money (4 exercises)*. Money Prodigy. https://www.moneyprodigy.com/h ow-to-teach-your-teenager-the-value-of-money/

Haagensen, E. (2023, March 2). *Common finance terms every newbie needs to know*. Investopedia. https://www.investopedia.com/articles/investing /061313/10-common-financial-terms-every-newbie-needs-know.asp

Hayes, A. (2022, March 25). *What is a red flag? Definition, use in investing, and examples*. Investopedia. https://www.investopedia.com/terms/r /redflag.asp

Hunt, D. (2022, July 27). *From clueless to clued in: Teaching teens about money*. Morgan Stanley; Morgan Stanley. https://www.morganstanley.c om/articles/teaching-teens-about-money

Huynh, L., & Merilles, M. (2021, April 16). *Money management: The importance of saving money as a teenager*. Talon. https://oakparktalon.org/12833/feature/money-management-th e-importance-of-saving-money-as-a-teenager/

Jain, P. (2022a, October 14). Importance of financial literacy for teens. *The Times of India*. https://timesofindia.indiatimes.com/blogs/voices/impo rtance-of-financial-literacy-for-teens/

Jain, P. (2022b, December 14). *7 reasons why teens should start earning money*. Funngro. https://www.funngro.com/blog/7-reasons-why-teens -should-start-earning-money

Kagan, J. (2023, April 4). *What is an ATM and how does it work?* Investopedia. https://www.investopedia.com/terms/a/atm.asp

Karr, A. (2023, July 5). *Why kids and teens should start saving money early*. Mydoh. https://www.mydoh.ca/learn/money-101/money-basics/ why-kids-and-teens-should-start-saving-money-early/

Knisley, M. (2023, May 16). *7 reasons you should make a budget: The benefits of budgeting*. InCharge Debt Solutions. https://www.incharge.o rg/financial-literacy/budgeting-saving/budgeting-benefits/

Kurt, D. (2022, February 9). *Emergency fund*. Investopedia. https://ww
w.investopedia.com/terms/e/emergency_fund.asp

Lake, R. (2022, October 19). *Budgets: Everything you need to know*.
The Balance. https://www.thebalancemoney.com/how-to-make-a-budg
et-1289587

Lake, R. (2023, March 3). *Teens and income taxes*. Investopedia. https://
www.investopedia.com/teens-and-income-taxes-7152618

Little, K. (2021, April 11). *Understanding risk and reward in investing*.
The Balance. https://www.thebalancemoney.com/understanding-risk-3
141268

Lobell, K. O. (2023, February 1). *Money foundations for kids: Compound
interest*. MoneyGeek.com. https://www.moneygeek.com/financial-plan
ning/compound-interest-for-kids/

Lokenauth, S. (2022, January 14). *Top 10 high-income skills
that teens can teach themselves from home*. The Teen Maga-
zine. https://www.theteenmagazine.com/top-10-high-income-skills-that
-teens-can-teach-themselves-from-home

Marquit, M. (2023, March 28). *What is net worth? Why does it matter?*
Forbes Advisor. https://www.forbes.com/advisor/investing/what-is-net
-worth/

Mehta, R. (2021, July 12). Money & relationship: What financial freedom
is right for your teen? Here are 5 rules to follow. *The Economic Times*.
https://economictimes.indiatimes.com/wealth/plan/money-relationship
-what-financial-freedom-is-right-for-your-teen-here-are-5-rules-to-follow/
articleshow/84288529.cms?from=mdr

Mitra, M. (2020, November 23). *Meet the teens saving for retirement*.
Money. https://money.com/teenagers-retirement-savings-roth-ira/

Muller, C. (2023, March 15). *Best investments for teens: 9 ways to get your
teens to invest*. Dough Roller. https://www.doughroller.net/investing/be
st-investments-for-teens/

Murray, S. (2023, April 4). *The benefits of teaching kids about money management early on*. Invstr. https://invstr.com/invstr-jr/the-benefits-of-tea
ching-kids-about-money-management-early-on/

Neidel, C. (2022, April 26). *Needs vs. wants: How to budget for both*. Nerd-Wallet. https://www.nerdwallet.com/article/finance/financial-needs-ver
sus-wants

Norris, E. (2022, June 14). *Top 10 most common financial mistakes*. Investopedia. https://www.investopedia.com/personal-finance/most-co
mmon-financial-mistakes/

O'Shea, B., & Schwahn, L. (2023, July 28). *Budgeting 101: How to budget money*. NerdWallet. https://www.nerdwallet.com/article/finance/how-t
o-budget

Oh, H. (2023, January 9). *These are the easiest ways to make money as a teen (and they actually work)*. Seventeen. https://www.seventeen.com/life/sc
hool/a42397406/how-to-make-money-as-teen/

Paris, D. (2023, May 3). *8 reasons to teach financial literacy to kids & teens*. Mydoh. https://www.mydoh.ca/learn/money-101/money-basics/
8-reasons-to-teach-financial-literacy-to-kids-teens/

Patel, I. (2020, October 15). *Benefits of earning money as a teen*. Medi-um. https://ishani2006patel.medium.com/benefits-of-earning-money-a
s-a-teen-ebe2a8e80139

Paul, H. (2022, December 13). *Diversification score, redflags and portfolio forecast: Our new updates make portfolio analysis quick and easy*. Blog by T i c k e r t a p e . https://www.tickertape.in/blog/diversification-score-redflags-and-portfol
io-forecast-our-new-updates-make-portfolio-analysis-quick-and-easy/

Pinto, M. L. (2022, August 11). *Why should teens be taught financial literacy?* Maddyness UK. https://www.maddyness.com/uk/2022/08/11
/why-should-teens-be-taught-financial-literacy/

Pragati Girdhar. (2022, February 11). *Top 10 ways to make money as teenagers*. Fyp Blog. https://www.fypmoney.in/blog/top-10-ways-to-ma
ke-money-as-teenagers/

Puharich, R. (2021a, October 16). *Loans for teens: What are they?* Teen-Learner. https://teenlearner.com/loans-for-teens/

Puharich, R. (2021b, October 17). *13 reasons to save money as a teenager*. TeenLearner. https://teenlearner.com/13-reasons-to-save-money-as-a-te

enager/

Quast, L. (2016, August 8). *10 tips to help you win every negotiation.* Forbes. https://www.forbes.com/sites/lisaquast/2016/08/08/10-tips-to -help-you-win-every-negotiation/

Rakoczy, C. (2023, June 16). *Why money is important: Benefits, downsides, and more.* LendEDU. https://lendedu.com/blog/why-money-is-import ant/

Rockwood, K. (2020, September 25). *Banking 101: Understanding how banks work.* Step. https://step.com/money-101/post/a-teens-guide-to-ba nking

Sabatier, G. (2023a, February 8). *18 ways teens can prepare for financial independence.* Millennial Money. https://millennialmoney.com/teens-fi nancial-independence/

Sabatier, G. (2023b, February 25). *Best investments for teenagers in 2023.* Millennial Money. https://millennialmoney.com/best-investments-for-t eenagers/

Sahu, S. (2022, September 12). *5 main reasons why you should start invest-ing young.* ET Money. https://www.etmoney.com/learn/mutual-funds/ 5-reasons-why-you-should-start-investing-young/

Sahu, S. (2023, January 31). *9 steps to achieve financial freedom.* ET Mon-ey. https://www.etmoney.com/learn/personal-finance/9-step-to-achieve -financial-freedom/

Schattenberg, P. (2023, August 1). *Five common money management mis-takes.* AgriLife Today. https://agrilifetoday.tamu.edu/2023/08/01/five-c ommon-money-management-mistakes/

Segal, T. (2023, July 1). *What is diversification? Definition as investing strategy.* Investopedia. https://www.investopedia.com/terms/d/diversific ation.asp

Smith, J. (2016, July 15). *Top 10 money myths held by teens and how to change them.* Aol. https://www.aol.com/2009/09/08/top-10-money-my ths-held-by-teens-and-how-to-change-them/

Soken-Huberty, E. (2023, July 22). *10 reasons why money is important.*

Open Education Online. https://openeducationonline.com/magazine/1 0-reasons-why-money-is-important

Strull, J. (2023, March 5). *Best debit cards for teens of 2023*. Verywell Family. https://www.verywellfamily.com/best-debit-cards-for-teens-5180261

Take Charge America Team. (2020, August 14). *What you need to know about bank accounts for teens*. Take Charge America. https://www.takechargeamerica.org/what-you-need-to-know-about -bank-accounts-for-teens/

Trivedi, A. (2022, October 25). *7 important financial terms you must teach your child*. Mintgenie. https://mintgenie.livemint.com/news/personal-finance/7-important-financial-terms-you-must-teach-your-child-151666348935092

Underwood, K. (2023, July 13). *How pursuing financial independence benefits you (even if you don't retire early)*. Due. https://due.com/pursuing-financial-independence-benefits/

Vaid, S. (2011, September 18). Money-teen your teenager! *The Economic Times*. https://economictimes.indiatimes.com/blogs/simplified-finance/money-teen-your-teenager/

Vohwinkle, J. (2022, July 5). *Should teens and college students have credit cards?* The Balance. https://www.thebalancemoney.com/should-teens-and-college-students-have-credit-cards-1289626

We Are Teachers Staff. (2023, March 14). *24 life skills every teen should learn*. We Are Teachers. https://www.weareteachers.com/life-skills-for-teens/

Webster, E. S. (2017, April 4). *7 tips for negotiating your salary*. Teen Vogue. https://www.teenvogue.com/story/how-to-negotiate-salary

Wei, J. (2015, December 18). *Carl Sandburg: Money is power*. Due. https://due.com/carl-sandburg-money-is-power/

White, A. (2022, September 8). *How to create a budget in 5 steps*. CNBC. https://www.cnbc.com/select/how-to-create-a-budget-guide/

Whiteman, L. (2023, July 24). *Investment guide for teens and parents with teens*. The Motley Fool. https://www.fool.com/investing/how-to-invest/

investing-for-teens/

Yong, S. (2023, April 25). *How to help kids and teens avoid impulse buying.* Mydoh. https://www.mydoh.ca/learn/blog/lifestyle/how-to-help-kids-and-teens-avoid-impulse-buying/

www.ingramcontent.com/pod-product-compliance
Lightning Source LLC
LaVergne TN
LVHW011206080426
835508LV00007B/636